Voyages of Discovery

Michael Gibson

Oxford University Press

Contents

Oxford University Press, Walton Street, Oxford OX2 6DP
Oxford   New York   Toronto
Delhi   Bombay   Calcutta   Madras   Karachi
Petaling Jaya   Singapore   Hong Kong   Tokyo
Nairobi   Dar es Salaam   Cape Town
Melbourne   Auckland

and associated companies in
Berlin   Ibadan

Oxford is a trademark of Oxford University Press

© Oxford University Press 1989

ISBN 0 19 913356 5

Printed in Great Britain at the Alden Press, Oxford

1 Myths, Legends, and Traveller's Tales

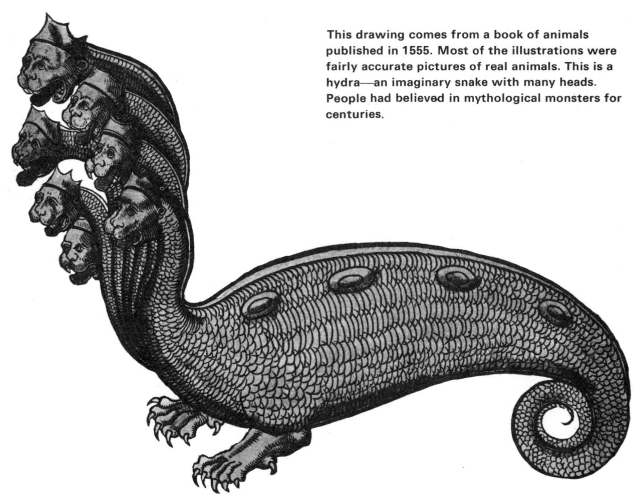

This drawing comes from a book of animals published in 1555. Most of the illustrations were fairly accurate pictures of real animals. This is a hydra—an imaginary snake with many heads. People had believed in mythological monsters for centuries.

Conrad Gesner, *Historia Animalium,* 1555. Bodleian Library

This picture of a Viking ship, from a manuscript of about 1200 A.D., was probably painted by a monk.

In the fifteenth century, the European's knowledge of the geography of the world was a tangled web of fact and fiction. The myths and legends of ancient and early medieval times as well as travellers' tales influenced people's idea of the world.

Stories about 'the Isles of the Blessed' were being told as long ago as 800 B.C. A man called Hesiod described how the gods rewarded outstanding mortals by carrying them west of the Pillars of Hercules (the Straits of Gibraltar) to the Islands of the Blessed where they lived in luxury for ever. These stories may go back even further than the ancient Greeks, and be based upon actual voyages into the Atlantic; in 1970, a traveller and archaeologist called Thor Heyerdahl built a boat of papyrus, just like the ancient Egyptians used. In it he crossed the Atlantic from North Africa to Barbados in the West Indies, and so proved that the Egyptians could have sailed across to Central America.

In Ireland, there are stories about St. Brenden or Brandan who seems to have been a real person. He was born about 484 A.D. and was taught mathematics and astronomy as well as Greek and Latin. According to the tales, he made two great voyages visiting Iceland, Greenland, Newfoundland and:

the fairest country that any man might see, it was so bright and clear that it was a heavenly sight to behold.

These stories were widely known and for ten centuries the 'Island of Saints' discovered by St. Brenden was marked on maps somewhere to the west of Ireland.

Later, the Vikings sailed westwards. Some of the sagas, long poems telling of the adventures of great heroes, describe how Eric the Red settled in Greenland and how Leif the Lucky reached the coast of North America, or Vinland, in the eleventh century. The two books of sagas which describe these events were written in the fourteenth century:

When Leif was ready, he set sail. His voyage was full of difficulties but in the end he discovered lands that had never been heard of before. They had fields of wild wheat and grapes. Maples grew among the trees, some of which were so big that houses were built out of them.

Historians believe that Leif landed somewhere in New England. Stones with Viking carvings on them have been found in North America. But the Viking settlements did not prosper and were abandoned so that all knowledge of them seems to have been lost. It is now certain that the Vikings reached America five hundred years before Columbus sailed across the Atlantic. Columbus' son Fernando in his biography of his father suggests that he knew something of the Vinland sagas; this would not be surprising for the stories were well known in the seaports of western Europe in the fifteenth century.

Another well-known legend is the story of the 'Lost Continent of Atlantis' which was first described by the Greek writer, Plato, in about 350 B.C.; he claimed that he had heard the story from the Egyptians. There was, he said, an enormous island beyond the Pillars of Hercules whose warrior inhabitants attacked the coasts of Europe and Asia without success. Then, there was a series of terrible earthquakes and the island sank beneath the sea.

In the fifth century B.C. Herodotus, a Greek writer, described in his *Histories* how the Phoenicians sailed from the Red Sea right round Africa:

Neco, the king of Egypt, ordered a fleet manned by Phoenicians to sail around the continent of Africa and to return to Egypt by means of the Straits of Gibraltar. They sailed southwards from the Gulf of Arabia; in the autumn, they landed on the coast, sowed some fields and waited there until the crop could be harvested. Having gathered in the grain, they put to sea once more and passed through the Pillars of Hercules in the second year of their voyage. They reached Egypt during the course of the third year.

By the fifteenth century his account was not believed and terrifying stories were told of the 'dread, green sea of darkness' which was said to lie beyond Cape Bojador, a cape in north-west Africa just south of the Canary Islands.

In the twelfth and thirteenth centuries, Europe was attacked by the Mongols from Central Asia and it seemed for a time that they would conquer the whole area. About the same time, rumours were heard of a great Christian king called Prester John who ruled a large part of Asia and who it was hoped would march to their rescue. Although this did not happen, the Mongols were defeated at Homs in 1281 by the Saracens and the belief in Prester John continued; after a time it was thought that he lived in Africa and ruled Abyssinia (Ethiopia). When the Portuguese reached the east coast of Africa, they spent a great deal of time trying to make contact with his successor; they were disappointed in their hopes.

The Mongol threat brought about a real increase in geographical knowledge as several European ambassadors searched for the emperor of the Mongols (or Tartars as they were also called) in Asia. Father John Carpini was sent off in 1245 by the Pope to find the Great Khan. He succeeded and wrote a brilliant account of what he saw in the *Book of the Tartars*. Here, he describes a war between the Mongols and Prester John:

The Mongol army marched against the Christians dwelling in Greater India, and the King of that country, known by the name of Prester John, came forth with his army to meet them. This Prester John had a number of hollow copper figures made resembling men, which were stuffed with combustibles and set upon horses; each one had a man mounted behind it with a pair of bellows to kindle the fire. At the beginning of the battle, these figures charged; the men riding behind them lit the combustibles and blew upon them with their bellows. When they exploded, the Mongol horses and men were set alight and the air was darkened with smoke.

A few years later, in 1253, King Louis IX of France sent Friar William of Rubruquis to Karakorum to convert the Khan; Friar William failed to do this, but he provided a vivid account of his travels through Asia. The most famous source of information about Asia and China was Marco Polo's *Travels*. They included many mistakes, exaggerations, and myths but both Henry the Navigator and Christopher Columbus carefully studied them.

In spite of the increase in geographical knowledge brought about by these journeys, the *Travels* of Sir John Mandeville (published in about 1370) were very popular and spread wildly inaccurate stories about the nature of the world. Here is part of his description of India:

In this land and in Ethiopia and in many countries, the men and women go to the waters and lay in them naked from 9 o'clock in the morning until gone noon because of the great heat of the sun. In this land, ships are made without nails or iron bands because there are rocks of Adamant (magnetic stone) in the sea which would draw the ships onto them.

He went on to describe Prester John and his kingdom:

This Emperor Prester John is Christian as is most of his kingdom. This Emperor has under his command 72 provinces, each ruled by a king. In the land of Prester John there are many marvels, amongst others there is a great sea of gravel and sand without a drop of water in it. It ebbs and

This engraving first appeared in a description of the world published in 1544

It was a very popular picture and was later included in several other books.

Sailors heard stories of monstrous men like these. Why do you think people believed in them?

MYTHS, LEGENDS, AND TRAVELLER'S TALES | 7

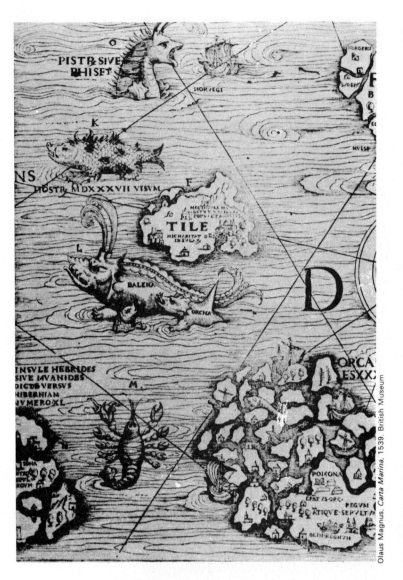

Sea monsters on part of a map by Olaus Magnus, published in 1639

flows like the sea and has great waves. That sea no man may pass, not by ship or any other means. Three days journey from this sea there are great hills out of which flows a great river that comes from Paradise and is full of precious stones and not a drop of water.

Even well educated men accepted some of these stories so it is not surprising that sailors believed most of them and added a mass of tales about the monsters of the deep— pictures of them can be seen on many medieval and early modern maps. Some of these stories may have been based on fact and not on ignorant superstition. Perhaps in those days, undisturbed by the engine noises and turbulence caused by modern ships, large sea creatures did rise to the surface of the sea.

Many sailors feared that they would be burnt black by the tropical sun or attacked by the deformed inhabitants of unknown lands. They thought that gorillas were one of these deformed races of men and so it was not difficult to believe in giants and men with their faces in their chests. The early explorers took a great interest in the native people they discovered and seem to have been surprised to find them normal.

The engravings opposite are from a book of animals, published in 1555. What is the animal in the pictures?

Compare these with a modern picture of the same animal. What mistakes did the sixteenth-century artist make?

What are the men doing in the top picture? What would they do with the flesh?

Does the bottom picture remind you of a Bible story?

Why do you think the anchor is stuck in the animal?

Do you find this or any of the other pictures frightening?
Can you make a picture of a more horrifying monster?
What twentieth-century monsters can you think of?

Do you think the old stories about the Atlantic encouraged or discouraged would-be explorers?

Why were Europeans so interested in Prester John? What did they hope to get from him?

Look carefully at the stories and legends. Which ones are obviously untrue? Which could be true? Which do you think are a mixture of fact and fiction?

Conrad Gesner, *Historia Animalium*, 1555. Bodleian Library

2 Maps and Charts

The ancient Greeks argued that the Earth was a sphere as long ago as the fifth century B.C.. Eratosthenes managed to measure the circumference of the world to within 100 miles of its actual size. Hipparchus introduced the idea of latitude and longitude.

Ptolemy collected and organised the geographical knowledge of his own day in a book called *Geographia*. Unfortunately, it included some serious mistakes: for example, he believed that the Indian Ocean was surrounded by land—the eastern and western sides were supposed to be joined to a great southern continent; he underestimated the size of the Earth by one-sixth; and thought that Asia extended much further east than it does.

This drawing shows Ptolemy's idea of the shapes of the continents

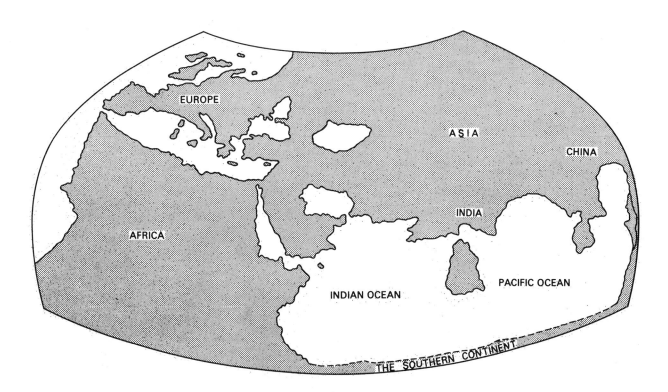

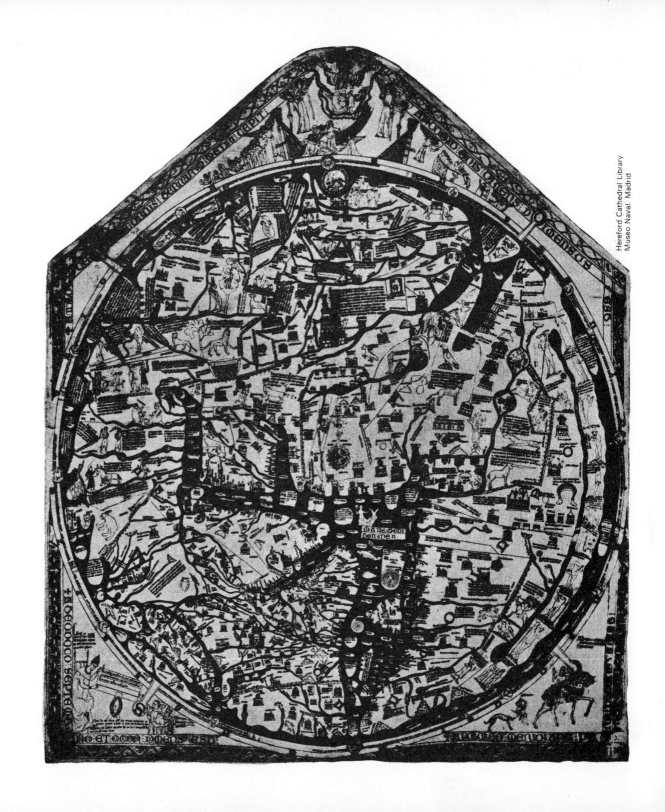

Paradise

INDIA

Ceylon

ASIA

China

Tower of Babel

Persian Gulf

Arabia

Red Sea

BABYLON

The
Ark

Sea of
Galilee

Black Sea

Cairo

EUROPE

Jerusalem

SOUTHERN AFRICA

Mediterranean Sea

Crete

AFRICA

Scotland

England

Wales

Sicily

Ireland

The ocean
surrounding
continents

Pillars of Hercules

The map on the left was made in 1290. The original is in Hereford Cathedral. This is one of the many maps made by monks in the Middle Ages.

The diagram above is a key to the 1290 map.

Which city is in the middle? Why do you think the monks put it there?

Which continents are shown? Which are left out altogether?

Why do you think the top of the map is pointing East and not North as in modern maps?

Would this map be of any use to a sailor?

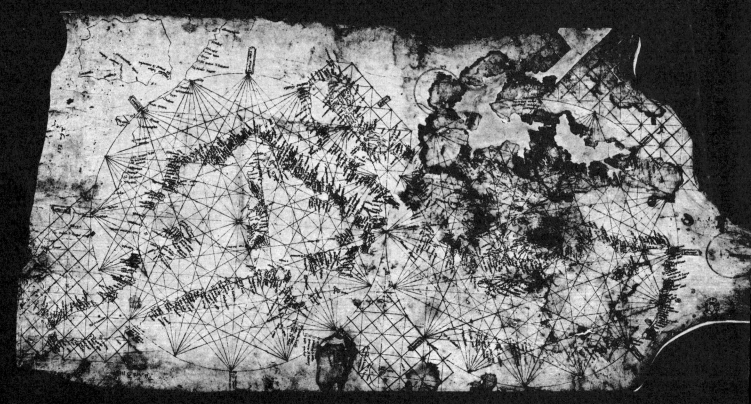

The earliest portolan chart, about 1300

In the Mediterranean area, sea charts or 'portolani' had been produced since the thirteenth century. These charts were drawn by sailors and contained practical information. No attempt was made to represent the curved surface of the earth on the flat map; the chart's shape was largely determined by that of the sheepskin on which it was drawn. No lines of latitude or longitude were marked but the whole chart was criss-crossed by thumb lines which radiated out from compass roses so that a sailor could work out the compass bearings he needed to sail from one place to another.

No details of the interior of the land were noted except for those landmarks that could be seen from the sea. These portolani were most beautifully drawn and decorated; a series of them dealing with a particular area were bound together to form an atlas. Copies of this could be made – by the end of the fourteenth century, there was a flourishing trade in portolani atlases throughout Western Europe.

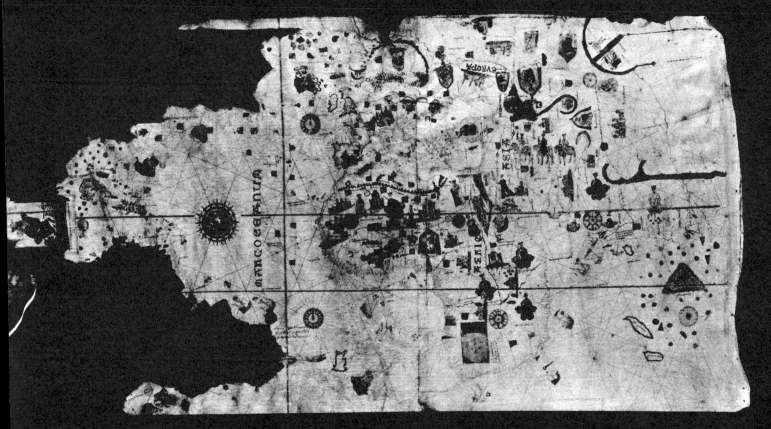

The first map which showed part of America, drawn by Juan de la Cosa, 1500

Many of the explorers made maps of their voyages. One of the few which survives is a sketch map of the north-west coast of Hispaniola, drawn by Columbus in December 1493 (see page 96).

The first map of America appeared in a chart of the world of 1500 made by Juan de la Cosa, the owner of the *Santa Maria* and one of Columbus' companions on the first and second voyages. He shows the mainland of America curving away to the north and south of the island of Cuba and Hispaniola. The equator and the Tropic of Cancer are marked on the map; this was unusual at that period.

By 1500, the Spanish and the Portuguese had official map-making institutions, which noted the new discoveries and added them to the charts that were used on their own expeditions.

A chart of the Indian Ocean by Diogo Homen, published in 1558, is printed in the booklet on Vasco da Gama's voyage (see page 85).

By the middle of the sixteenth century, maps of the world showed the outlines of the greater part of the continents. Below is Lopo Homen's world map of 1554.

These map makers ignored the fact that the earth's surface is curved and that the meridians of longitude move closer together as they approach the north and south poles, so navigators could not plot courses on their maps. Mercator solved this problem by making all the parallels of latitude

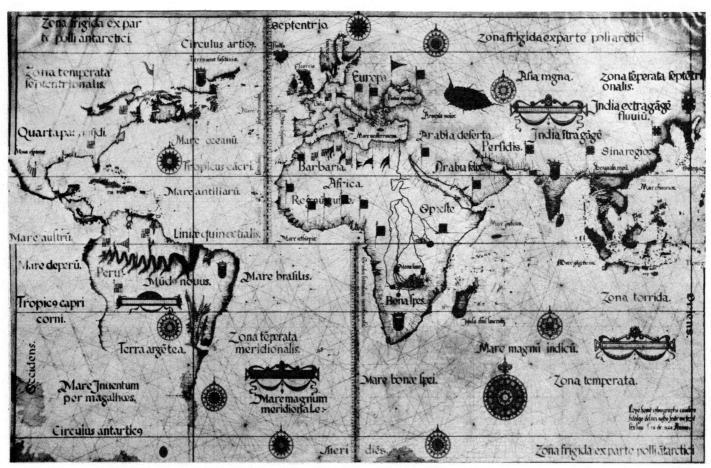

Lopo Homen's world map, 1554

the same length as the equator and by gradually increasing the spaces between them. This distorts the shape of the countries but enables a sailor to work out his compass course by drawing a straight line from one place to another.

Now, map makers were able to produce sea-charts to guide sailors across unknown seas.

Here is a drawing of Mercator's world map of 1569.

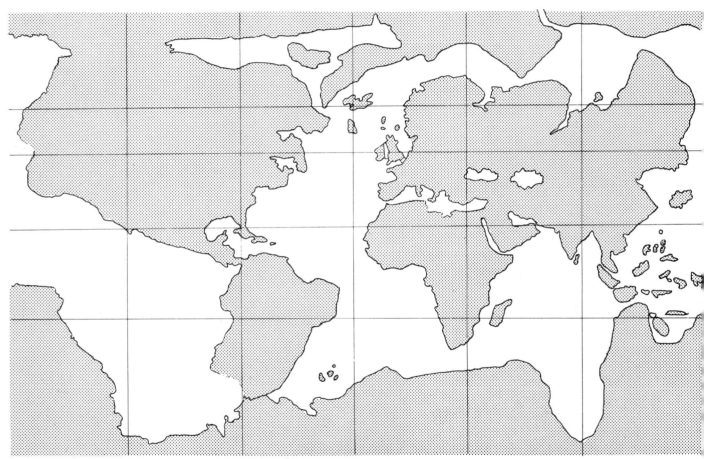

A simplified drawing of Mercator's world map, 1569

Here are some of the instructions given to the English navigators of 'a voyage of Discovery to Beyond Nova Zembla' in 1588:

Seek to amend the Plat (the map or chart) you have by making many observations—and thus make a new one.

1. Observe the Latitude in as many places as possible and note the place.
2. Work out with your compass how the land doth lie from promontory to promontory and use your judgement for what lieth between each point.
3. Draw the biting in of the land as well as the outlying points and headlands, and give them apt names. And mark on the drawing whether the land be high cliffs, low land, shady hills or whatever.
4. In passing (along the coast), keep the lead* going, sounding at least every glass, and note the depth and the nature of the seabed.
5. Observe the flowing and ebbing of the sea and how the tide do set and what force the tide hath as far as you can judge.
6. Use, as taught, the instruments, I send you for they will aptly serve your purpose.
7. Take paper and ink and keep a continuous journal daily that all may be seen and read at your return.
8. Note as many things as you can learn of the peoples wheresoever you may be.
9. By diligently observing the orders twill be easy for you to make a plat and description of your voyage.
Thus God prosper your voyage. Amen.

Questions to consider.

Was Ptolemy's *Geographia* any help to the early explorers?

How useful to a sailor were the maps made by the churchmen in the Middle Ages?

What were the uses of the Portolan Charts?

Compare the map on page 16 with the drawing of the map on page 11. What had geographers learnt by 1554? What had they still to learn?

Why was it so difficult to produce useful sea charts before the second half of the sixteenth century?

As you read about each voyage, keep in mind the idea of the world map that the explorers had before they set out

* See A6 on Navigation.

3 The Ship

The cog

In Northern Europe during the Middle Ages, the most common vessel was a single-masted ship with a large sail—the 'cog'.

This drawing of a cog is copied from a picture by a medieval French artist.

It was 'clinker built'; that is the edges of the upper planks projected over the lower ones like the tiles on a roof.

Stern view of a cog

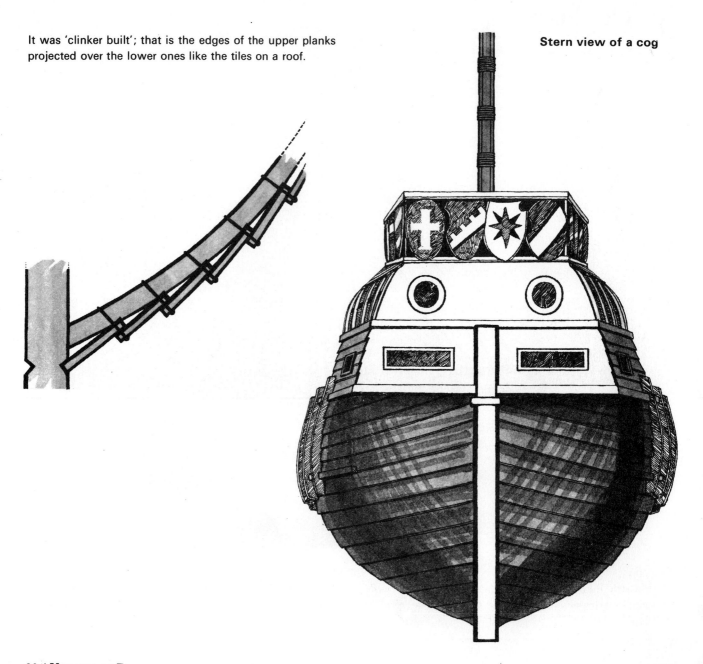

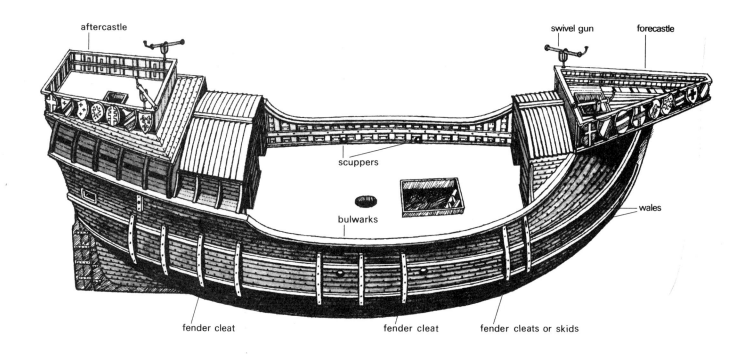

aftercastle

swivel gun

forecastle

scuppers

bulwarks

wales

fender cleat

fender cleat

fender cleats or skids

'Fender Cleats' or 'skids', and 'wales', protected the hull from damage when bumping against quays and so on. 'Bulwarks' prevented the deck from flooding, and 'scuppers' kept the deck drained.

The 'forecastle' and 'aftercastle' were defensive positions from which archers and handgun men could shoot down on their opponents.

Section through a cog

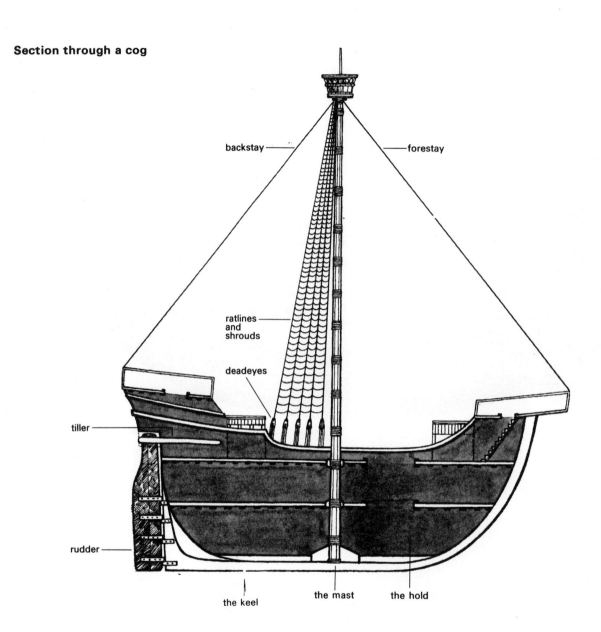

backstay

forestay

ratlines
and
shrouds

deadeyes

tiller

rudder

the keel

the mast

the hold

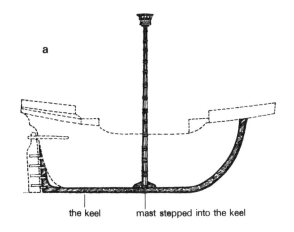

a

the keel   mast stepped into the keel

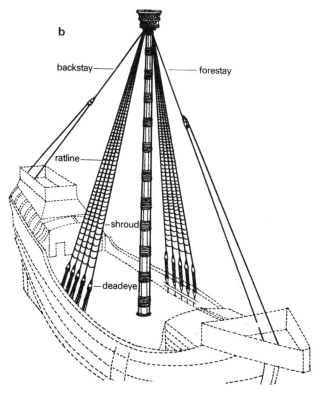

b

backstay —   — forestay

ratline

shroud

deadeye

As the mast was often as long as the ship itself, it had to be 'stepped' into the keel so that it did not overstrain the framework of the vessel when the sail was set (diagram **a**).

The mast was supported by fixed ropes, 'shrouds' and 'stays'. 'Ratlines' were small pieces of rope stretched across the shrouds to make a ladder for the sailors to climb aloft. (diagram **b**).

The stays and shrouds were tightened and slacked off by adjusting the 'lanyards'. The end of the rope from the rigging was wrapped round a wooden block (see below). A second block was attached to the bulwark by a metal strap. Cords, called 'lanyards' bound the two blocks together, threaded through holes in the blocks. The length of the lanyards could easily be altered to tighten or slacken the rope (diagram **c**).

The ship was steered by a long 'tiller', which passed through an open 'port' in the stern, and was fixed to the head of a wooden rudder (diagram **d**). In bad weather several men would be needed to keep the tiller straight and hold the ship on its course.

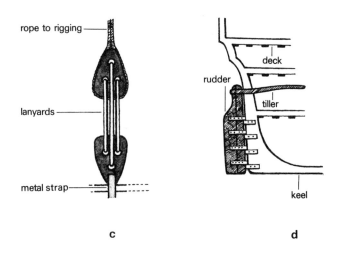

rope to rigging

lanyards

metal strap

deck

rudder

tiller

keel

c   **d**

The rigging of the sail on a cog

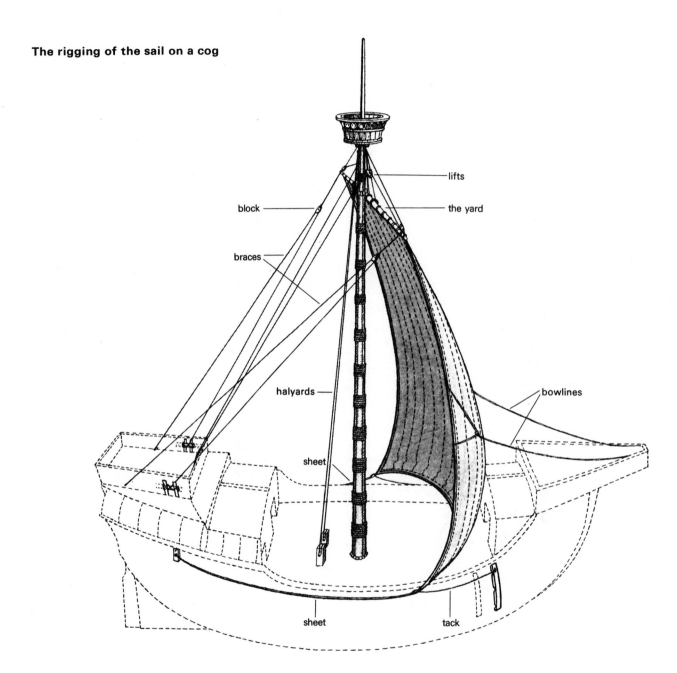

lifts

block

the yard

braces

halyards

bowlines

sheet

sheet

tack

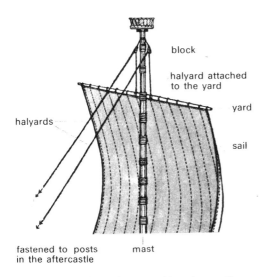

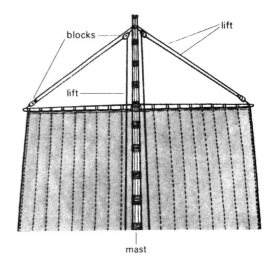

The sail was hoisted up into position by pulling on the 'halyards'.

In addition 'lifts' supported the yard and steadied its ends.

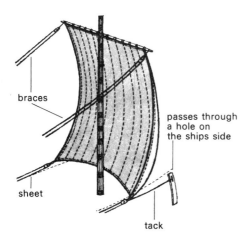

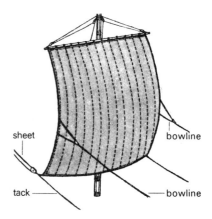

Sailors 'hauled on the braces' to swing the sail round until it filled with wind. The lower ends of the sail were pulled forward by 'tacks' and aft by 'sheets'.

'Bowlines' kept the sail 'close to the wind'. They were ropes attached to the sides of the sail.

Enlarging the sail area with bonnets

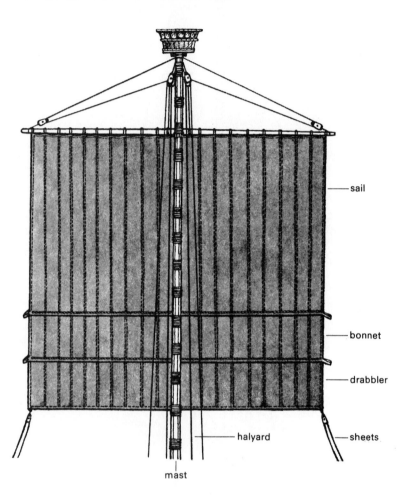

When winds were light, the size of the sail was increased by lacing 'bonnets' to the foot of the mainsail; sometimes further strips called 'drabblers' were added, so that the most could be made of the lightest breeze.

Reefing the sail

Furling the sail

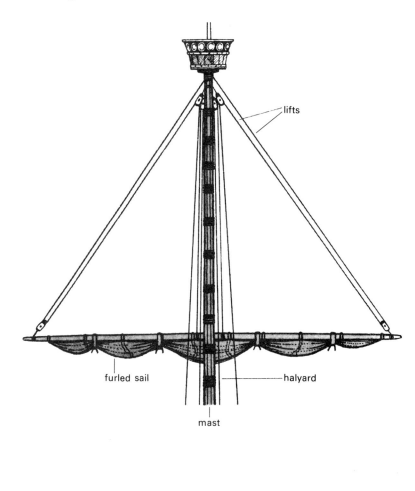

reef points

lifts

furled sail

halyard

mast

If, on the other hand, strong winds blew, the area of the mainsail had to be reduced by 'reefing'—the bottom of the sail was rolled up and fastened by 'reef points'.

During gales, the mainyard was lowered to the deck where the sail was 'furled'; it was folded up and lashed to the yard. The ship sailed before the wind under 'bare poles'.

Later, shipwrights introduced a small mast projecting forward from the bows called the 'bowsprit' which carried a small 'sprit' sail; this did not make the ship much faster but enabled it to manoeuvre more easily.

A second or 'fore' mast was added and then a third, or 'mizzen' mast, in about 1450. By 1500 some ships had four masts and a bowsprit.

The bowsprit

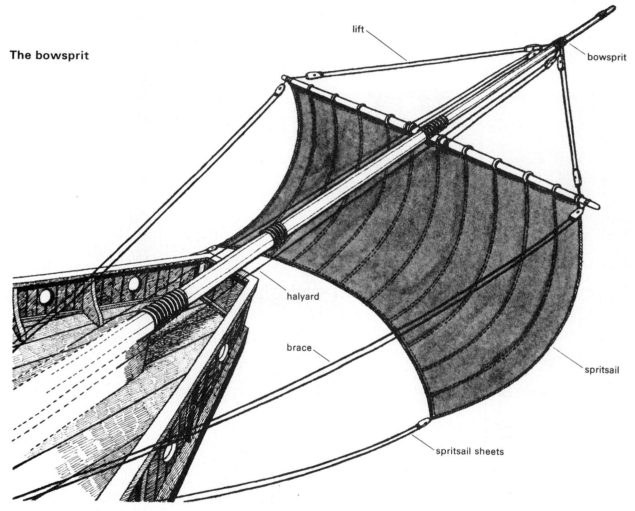

lift

bowsprit

halyard

brace

spritsail

spritsail sheets

The carrack

A single square sail on each mast did not provide enough power for these large vessels, so 'topsails' were rigged above the mainsails.

The great sails which drove the ship along were known as the 'courses'. These ships were called 'carracks'.

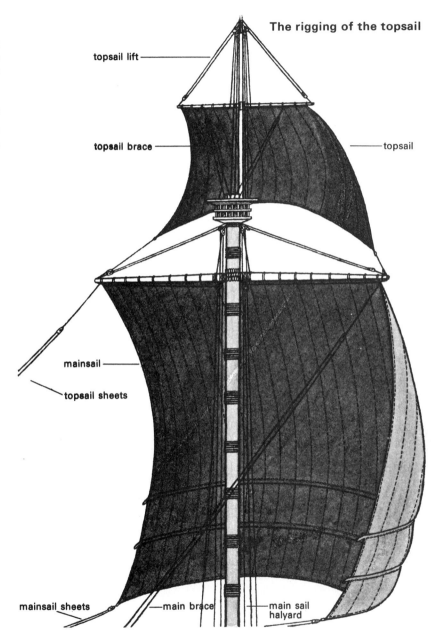

The rigging of the topsail

topsail lift

topsail brace

topsail

mainsail

topsail sheets

mainsail sheets — main brace — main sail halyard

Reconstruction of the caravel

The caravel

The people of Spain and Portugal perfected a vessel called the 'caravel'. This was a completely different kind of ship from the carrack. It had a much lighter hull and was 'carvel' built, that is each plank is nailed edge to edge with those above and below it.

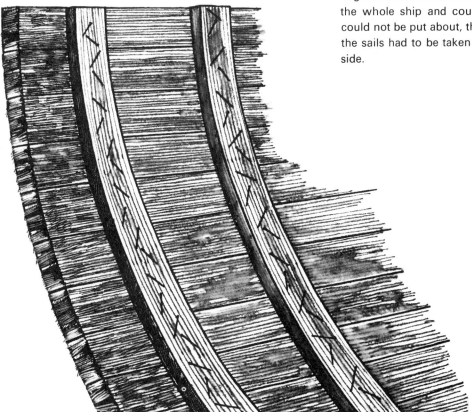

There was no forecastle and bowsprit, and the masts were stepped well back in the ship. As there were no ratlines, the crew had to use a ladder to climb the mast. The main difference was in the shape of the sails; the caravel carried 'lateen' sails which were triangular and were rigged obliquely on the masts. They were handy and fast and suited to coasting voyages. Cadamosto, one of Henry the Navigator's captains, said that they were 'the best ships that sail the sea' and 'they could go anywhere'.

But large caravels were not suitable for long voyages. Large crews were needed to work the ship; the sails were large and difficult to handle—the mainyard was as long as the whole ship and could not be furled easily. The ship could not be put about, that is turned round, easily because the sails had to be taken down and re-rigged on the other side.

A model of the 'Santa Maria', Columbus' flagship

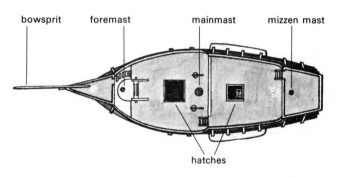

Bird's-eye view of the 'Santa Maria'

The nao

Gradually, the best features of the North European and Spanish ships were brought together in a new ship, the 'nao'. Columbus' flagship, the *Santa Maria*, was a nao. Contemporary evidence is scanty, but much work has been done on reconstructing this ship, and historians can now guess what she looked like.

The *Santa Maria* was an ordinary merchant vessel and had not been specially built to cross the Atlantic. Her hull was stubby and broad of beam (page 45): she seems to have been about $78\frac{1}{2}$ feet from stem to stern (front to back), her keel was $55\frac{1}{2}$ feet long and her beam was 26 feet. She was carvel built and protected by skids and fender cleats. She had a raised forecastle, a lower waist and a quarter and poop deck, one raised above the other. She carried three masts and a bowsprit; her sail plan was described by Columbus himself in an entry in the Log Book of his first voyage.

I let them set all sails, the main course with two bonnets, the fore course, the spritsail, the mizzen, the topsail and the boatsail on the half deck.

There was one boat and probably only one cannon. The crew consisted of some 38 or 40 officers and sailors. Columbus does not seem to have been pleased with her performance and said 'she was not suited for voyages of discovery'.

Many of the ships involved in the most famous expeditions were in poor condition. A contemporary said of Magellan's ships in 1518.

They are very old and patched and I should be sorry to sail for the Canaries in them, for their ribs are as soft as butter.

The development of the 'nao' made the voyages of discovery possible. The larger hulls could carry the necessary men and stores, and were better able to withstand rough weather. The divided sail plan provided greater power while the lateen sail on the mizzen and the sprit sail made them easier to handle.

Suggestions for practical work

1. Trace the development of ships—the 'cog', the 'carrack', the 'caravel' and the 'nao'—either by a series of models or by a set of large, labelled diagrams.

   OR Make large models or labelled diagrams of selected features of the ships such as their hulls, sail plans, etc. Sails can be cut out of cloth or canvas and rigged on poles.

2. If a large water trough is available or can be made, small model ships can be sailed, rigged in different ways, with an electric fan as a wind source in this way, the strengths and weaknesses of the different types of vessel can be observed at first hand.

Questions to consider

1. What is the difference between 'clinker' and 'carvel' built ships?
2. How did shipwrights (pages 35-50) protect the ship's fabrics from being damaged in collisions with quays or other ships?
3. What were 'dead-eyes' used for?
4. When were 'bonnets' used? What difference did they make?
5. What is the difference between 'reefing' and 'furling' sails?
6. Why were 'topsails' introduced?
7. How did 'spritsails' improve a ship's sailing qualities?
8. Make a list of the differences between the 'cog' and the 'caravel'.
9. What made the 'naos' suitable for sailing across the oceans of the world?

A note on tunnage

Historians have had great difficulty in working out the actual size of the great explorer's ships as there were many local variations in the unit of measurement, the 'tun' or 'ton'. During the Middle Ages, it had become customary to describe the size of a ship by the number of barrels of wine or tuns that it could carry. Unfortunately, an English tun was not the same as a Spanish or a Venetian one; indeed, the size of the barrel could change from port to port. No serious attempt was made to develop a method of calculating tonnage according to the dimensions of the ship until much later, so many reconstructions of the early explorers' ships are based on our knowledge of a number of ships of their type and some inspired guesswork.

Drawings by Charles Sutton

The galleon

The galleon was a further development of the nao, made as a result of experience gained crossing the great oceans of the world.

This is an engraving by Frans Huys of a sixteenth century drawing of a galleon by Pieter Brueghel the elder.

National Maritime Museum

4 Shipbuilding

Matthew Baker. *Fragments of Ancient English Shipwrightry*, 1586. Pepysian Library. Magdalene College. Cambridge

The shipbuilders chose a plot of land close to a stretch of sheltered water, on a river, or the seashore, and built a storehouse, sheds, and a drawing office.

This is a scene in a shipwright's drawing office, from a manuscript by an Elizabethan shipwright Matthew Baker. It shows two men preparing a 'sheer plan', a design of the lengthwise lines of a ship.

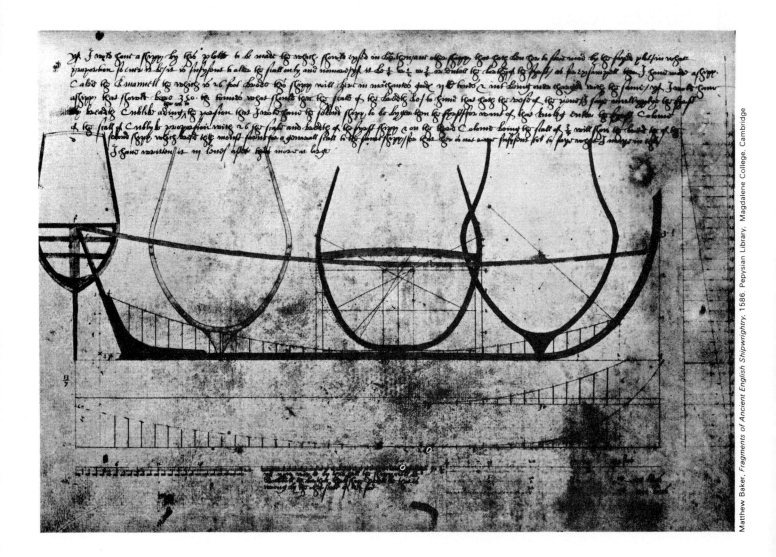

Matthew Baker, *Fragments of Ancient English Shipwrightry*. 1586. Pepysian Library. Magdalene College. Cambridge

These cross sections are from a page of Matthew Baker's manuscript.

The shipwrights designed a series of cross sections through the body of the ship, showing the shape of the hull at different points.

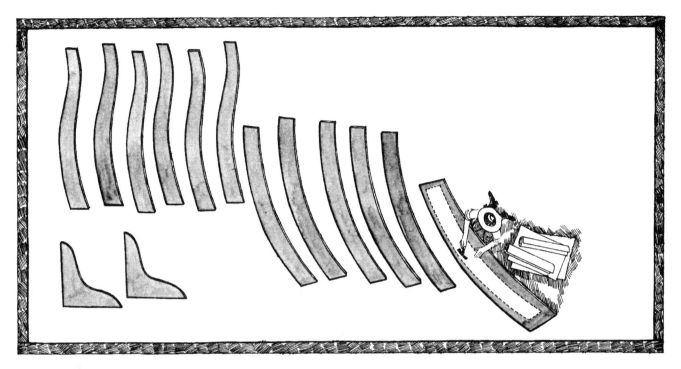

A craftsman making templates on the floor of the moulding loft; a view from above

When they had finished their small scale plans, they re-drew them with chalk full size on a huge wooden floor called the 'moulding loft'. Then they tacked thin wooden battens down on the chalk drawings and shaped them to make 'templates' for all the various parts of the ship's framework. These were then nailed on to the rough timbers as patterns to cut out the frames or ribs of the ship.

Oak was the best wood for ship building because of its strength. Men searched the forests for suitable trees whose natural curved shape fitted those required by the shipbuilders; the sawyers did not want to cut out shapes against the grain as this would reduce the natural strength of the wood.

When a shipbuilder looked at a tree, he saw a series of parts ready to be cut out as the drawing shows. Find a real oak tree. Try to draw it and mark the branches as the artist has done in this diagram.

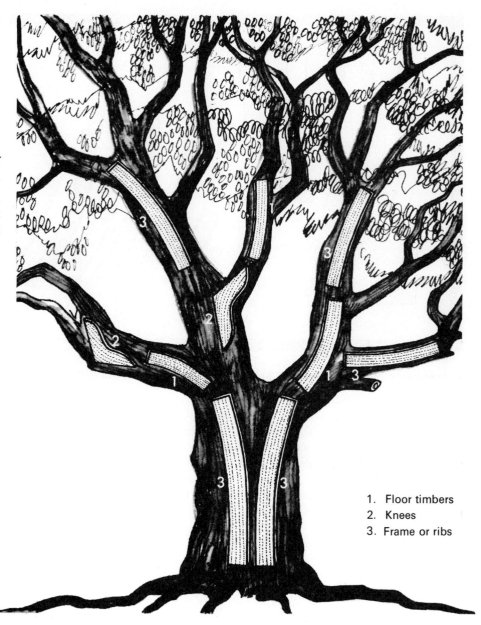

1. Floor timbers
2. Knees
3. Frame or ribs

Once the wood had been cut, the sawyers, carpenters and ship-wrights set to work nailing their moulds onto the timber and fashioning the ribs, knees and so on. The wood was cut with the grain and so there was not a straight line or edge in the ship.

A pit was dug and the tree trunks placed over it. A long two-handled saw was operated by two men—the one on top of the log was the 'top sawyer' and the one in the pit underneath was the 'bottom sawyer'.

The pieces were trimmed and shaped with an 'adze', an implement about a metre long, which looked like a garden hoe but had a longer and sharper blade. The craftsman stood on the timber and chopped off large shavings. He worked towards his foot. The trimmed wood was smooth and undulating.

The saw pit

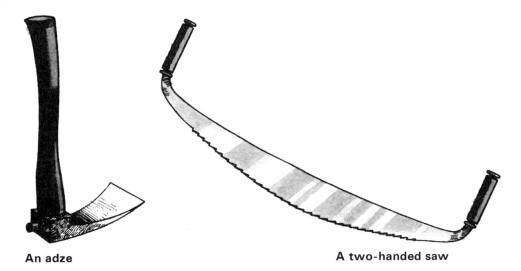

An adze

A two-handed saw

The 'keel' was laid on guiding blocks near the waterside.

'Stem and stern posts' were fitted into it. The stem curved up to provide a cutting edge to help the ship shoulder its way through the sea, while the stern was straight to provide firm support for the rudder.

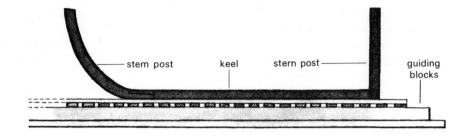

stem post   keel   stern post   guiding blocks

'Floor timbers' were bolted into the keel, and formed the basis for the great 'ribs'.

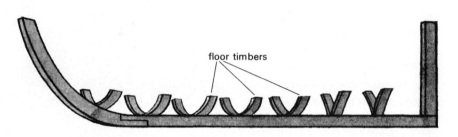

floor timbers

The 'keelson', an inner keel, was fitted above the keel and the floor timbers.

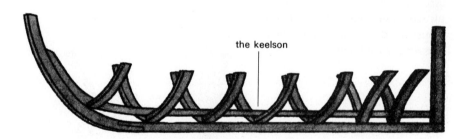

the keelson

The ribs, each made up of several lengths of wood, were completed to produce the curved shape of the ship (see page 44).

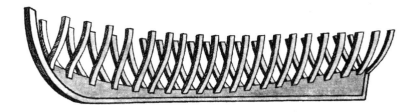

Stout timbers called 'wales' stretched from stem to stern.

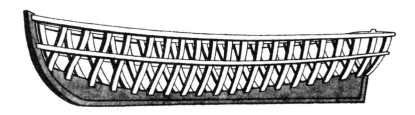

Beams were laid across the ribs, and secured to them by 'knees' (see page 45).

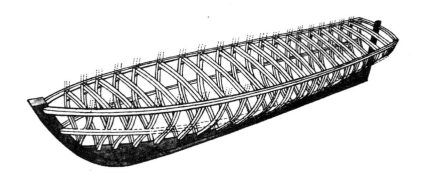

This comes from an engraving illustrating the building of Noah's Ark. The artist Jan Sadeler shows the methods of ship building which he saw in the early sixteenth century.

How many different tools can you name? What was the main function of each?

Describe all the work going on in the picture. Notice details in the background as well as in the foreground.

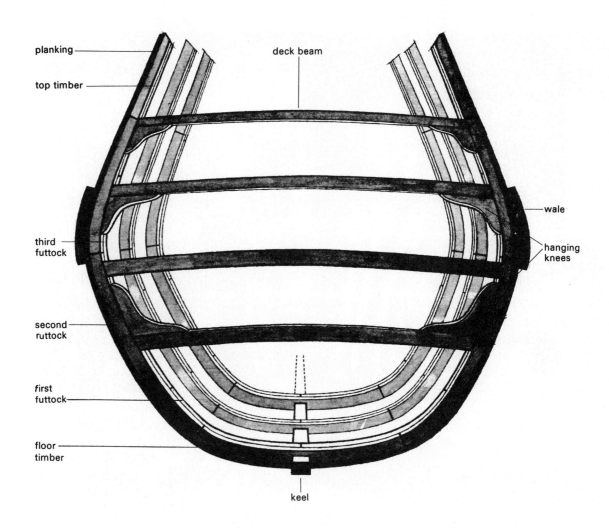

planking

top timber

deck beam

third
futtock

second
ruttock

first
futtock

floor
timber

wale

hanging
knees

keel

A cross section showing how the ship's hull was constructed

The ribs were made up of several lengths of wood, known as 'futtocks', which fitted against each other to provide the curved shape of the ship.

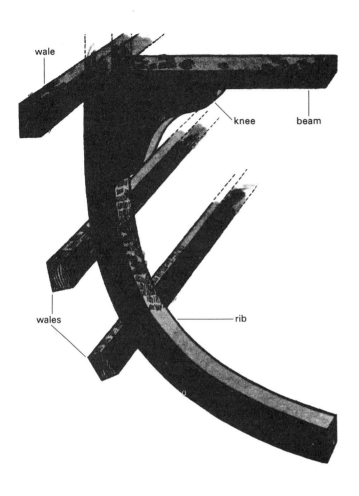

wale

knee

beam

wales

rib

The junction of the rib and deck beam

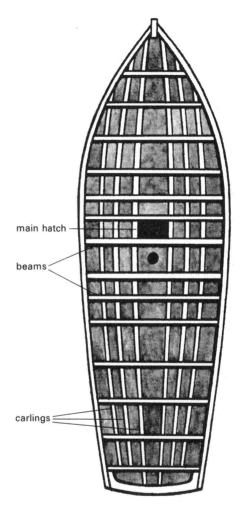

main hatch

beams

carlings

A view from above, showing the beams before the deck planking was added

'Carlings' were set between the beams and provided the support for the deck.

Notice that the beams were closer together nearer the mast where the pressure would be greatest.

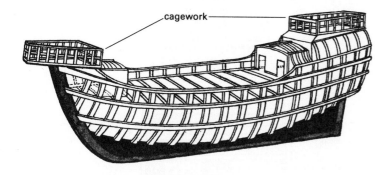

cagework

Timber frameworks were constructed where the stern and forecastles would be.

When the frame was complete, the planking was added; underwater wooden pegs or 'treenails' were used to fasten the planks to prevent rusting while iron nails were used above the waterline—often they were made in the shipyard.

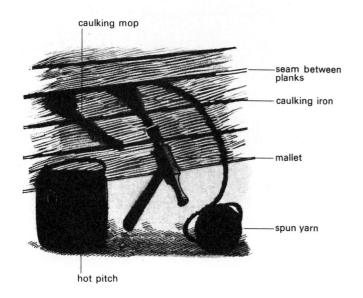

caulking mop

seam between planks

caulking iron

mallet

spun yarn

hot pitch

It was not usual to sheath the bottom of ships with copper sheets until the second half of the eighteenth century; so the planking was fully exposed to the sea. The gaps between the planks were caulked, filled with spun yarn, hemp or oakum (loose fibres from old ropes) which was hammered home and then the ship's bottom was painted with pitch. The superstructure was well painted to prevent rotting.

The 'stepping' of the mast

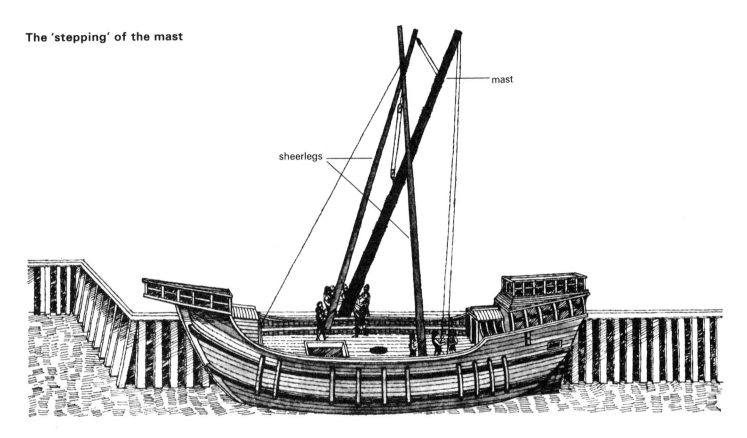

The mast or masts had to be 'stepped' into 'shoes' made out of blocks of wood. The mainmast, which was often as long as the ship itself, had to be stepped into the keel. It was swung into position by sheerlegs, a kind of primitive crane, and a slip could send it plunging through the ship's bottom.

Foremasts and mizzen masts were smaller and had to stand less strain so that they were stepped in shoes resting on one of the decks. All the masts had to be supported by a number of ropes: the fore and back 'stays' and the 'shrouds'.

The rake (the angle of the mast to the deck) of the mast could be changed by altering the length of the ropes and the position of the shoes to improve the performance of the ship in different conditions.

Now, the ship could be fitted out. The masts were rigged with shrouds and ratlines, the rope ladders, and the spars were fitted. The sails were cut out and hand sewn. Usually a second set would be made at the same time—Magellan insisted that each of his ships should have a complete reserve set of sails before setting out on his voyage round the world.

The vessel could not be safely sailed until ballast had been taken aboard. Many new ships were lost in home waters because their ballast had not been properly arranged. Ballast usually consisted of sand and shale; the performance of a ship could be drastically improved by altering the lie of the ballast. In the same way, the greatest care had to be taken over the loading of provisions and cargo to preserve the ship's best trim; not only did this enable her to sail faster but it made her easier to handle in stormy seas.

Finally, the new ship was ready for sea. It had to carry materials for repairs: timbers, spare spars, ropes and cordage, sails and canvas, nails and pitch, and so on.

In stormy seas it was an easy thing to lose a mast and then the ship would be crippled unless a temporary, or 'jury' mast could be rigged. Then there was always the chance of fighting at sea and being seriously damaged. Craftsmen as well as materials were needed, and the carpenter, the sailmaker, etc. were valued members of every crew.

Sailing ship beached for careening

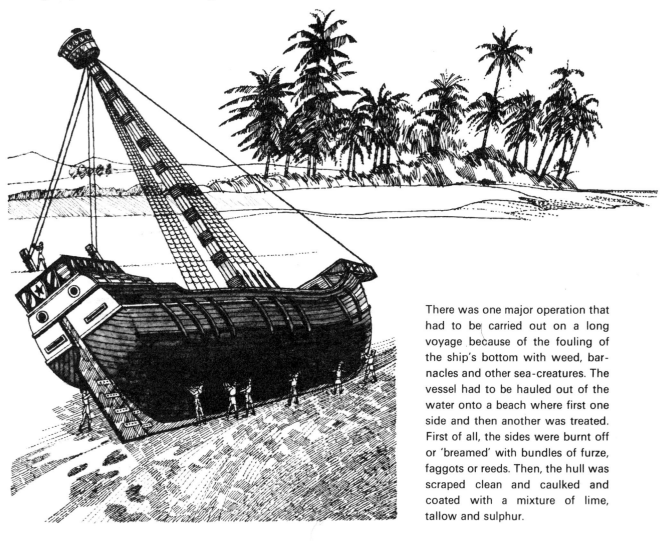

There was one major operation that had to be carried out on a long voyage because of the fouling of the ship's bottom with weed, barnacles and other sea-creatures. The vessel had to be hauled out of the water onto a beach where first one side and then another was treated. First of all, the sides were burnt off or 'breamed' with bundles of furze, faggots or reeds. Then, the hull was scraped clean and caulked and coated with a mixture of lime, tallow and sulphur.

Suggestions for practical work

1. Make your own sheer plans for an ocean-going ship. Draw up list of points to be borne in mind in the design of the vessel.
2. Make a series of drawings or models showing the various stages in the construction of a sailing ship.
3. Make drawings or models of the shipyards, storehouses, etc. Shipbuilding scenes can be shown in dioramas; the models can be made out of wood or cardboard; the background scenes can be painted or made up of cuttings from magazines and posters; ordinary cardboard or wooden boxes can be used as diorama cases.
4. Make drawings or a model of a cross-section through a ship. See Chapter 5 for conditions on board ship.
5. Make a series of strip-cartoon pictures to illustrate the work of the various craftsmen.

Questions to consider

1. What were templates?
2. How was the 'moulding floor' used?
3. How did the shipwrights manage to make use of the natural strength of the wood they were using?
4. Make a list of all the different craftsmen who would be needed to build a ship.
5. Why were 'treenails' used to peg the planks below the waterline?
6. Why was it necessary to 'caulk' and 'pitch' the bottom of the ship?
7. What was ballast? Why was it necessary?
8. Why was it necessary to 'careen' a ship regularly?
9. Which were the most dangerous moments in the construction of a ship?

Drawings by Charles Sutton

5 Officers, Crew, and Shipboard Conditions

Lisbon harbour in about 1600

De Bry *Voyages.* c.1600. National Maritime Museum

The Captain was the official commander of the ship. He ruled the entire community, kept the muster book which contained a list of the names of the crew and their jobs and an account of the stores. He was responsible for the discipline and had the power of life and death over his crew. Magellan executed or marooned the ringleaders of the mutiny at San Julian and severe physical punishments were meted out for minor crimes.

Section through a sailing ship

Often the navigation of the vessel would be in the hands of a Master; William Barents occupied this position on his last voyage. The Master was the second-in-command and a man of great importance. He was responsible for the working of the ship and for adjusting the sails to every change in the wind.

In addition, he would take 'shots' of the sun or stars to ascertain the ship's latitude, and gauge her speed through the water to work out her longitude. He had the course to set and the Log, a day to day record of the voyage, to keep.

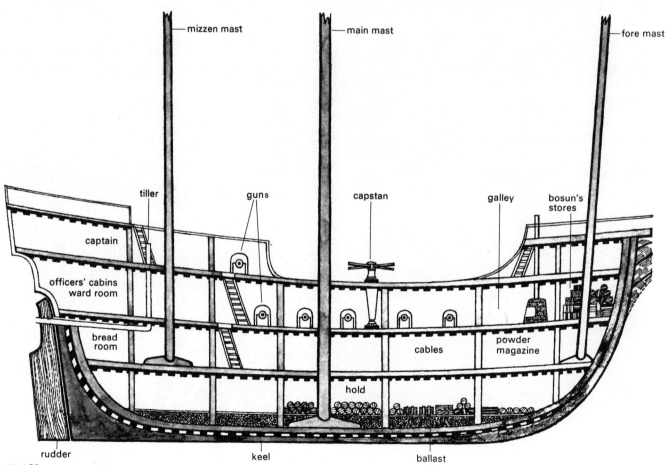

mizzen mast — main mast — fore mast

tiller — guns — capstan — galley — bosun's stores

captain

officers' cabins ward room

bread room — cables — powder magazine

hold

rudder — keel — ballast

The most important of the non-commissioned officers was the Boatswain or 'Bosun' who was responsible for the upkeep of the ship's rigging, her sails, her anchors, and boats. He was in charge of hoisting and lowering the anchor—difficult operations because of the size of the anchor and the anchor cable. It was too thick to bend round the capstan so a smaller continuous rope had to be attached to it as soon as it appeared through the hawsehole—this was known as a 'messenger' and was wound in by the capstan while the cable was coiled away below. The process was carried out time and again until all the cable had been got in. The boys who attached the smaller ropes to the cable or nipped them became known as 'nippers'. The Bosun carried a silver whistle on a chain around his neck and he blew shrilly to attract the sailors' attention before repeating the Master's orders.

Below the Bosun was the Coxswain or Coxon who had charge of the Captain's boat and steered it. He acted as the Bosun's deputy and also carried a whistle.

Apart from these active sailors, there were the specialists. The Gunner was the most important of these: he was in charge of the guns and responsible for their maintenance; on occasions, he might share the direction of a battle with the Captain. The Purser was 'an able clerk' who kept the ship's accounts and issued the provisions while his assistant, the Steward, supervised the ship's candles and breadroom. Although not a sailor, the clerk or Purser could occupy an important position on board ship as one of the few men who could write; the Purser on Hudson's last voyage was one of the leaders of the mutineers. The hold of the ship was stowed and kept clean by the Quartermasters. There was usually a surgeon on board, and there were many other craftsmen who served the ship such as the Carpenter, the Sailmaker, the Caulkers, the Coopers, and so on.

Taking up the anchor

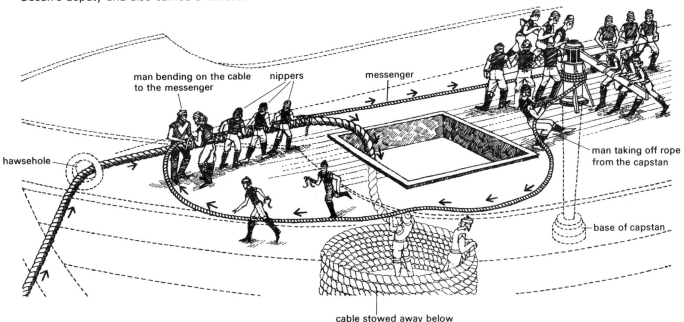

man bending on the cable to the messenger   nippers   messenger

hawsehole

man taking off rope from the capstan

base of capstan

cable stowed away below

Beneath the officers, the non-commissioned officers and the craftsmen came the ordinary sailors who did most of the work on board ship whether handling the ropes, reefing the sails, moving the cargo or firing the guns. It was often difficult to obtain a sufficient number of sailors to man the ships especially if it were known that they would be sailing to unknown seas and lands. Sometimes 'persuasion' was used. When Columbus arrived at the little port of Palos in 1492, he had a Royal Order commanding the inhabitants to provide him with ships and crew—this partly explains his difficulties with his crew on this voyage; even his captains had been forced to accompany him. An alternative was to keep the true destination of the fleet a secret as Magellan did.

Large crews were required to work these ships and to provide all the specialist skills needed on a long voyage. There was usually a man to every two tons of shipping (see Chapter 3) which meant that below decks were very over-crowded. Men slept up on deck in fine weather and below in rickety cots in foul. Hammocks were first found by Columbus amongst the Indians of the Caribbean but they were not adopted by sailors until the sixteenth century and then by no means always. Belongings were stowed away in seaman's chests which served as tables and chairs and much else besides.

The seaman's clothes were made of coarse, hardwearing materials like canvas. They were usually made at sea by the men themselves and were rightly called 'slops'.

In the winter, long sack-like woollen dresses were worn. Whatever the time of year, the clothes were rarely washed so that they became infested with vermin and were the source of sores because of their rough texture.

In stormy, wet weather, clothes were saturated with sea-water and could not be dried as all fires had to be extinguished in rough weather.

Sailors in Elizabethan costume. Details from the frontispiece to a sixteenth-century book on navigation.

details from Waghenaer's *Mariners' Mirror*, 1588. photo P. Davy

The sailor's diet was mainly salt meat and fish, ship's biscuit or bread, and beer or wine—water was not drunk until all the beer or wine had been consumed. Fresh food and vegetables were quickly used up in the first weeks of the voyage so that the crew would have to survive on this diet until the ship put in to land. The crew was divided into 'messes' for their meals. A Spanish sailor described such a scene:

In a twinkling, out poured the whole ship's company saying 'Amen' on their way, and sat down on the deck around what served as a table, the bosun at the head with the gunner on his right, some sailors sat cross-legged, some with legs stretched out, others squatted or reclined in any posture they chose; and without pausing for grace whipped out their knives or daggers and fell upon their food.

The diet was varied with butter, cheese, onions, dried peas, and beans, and even candles in the case of Hudson's mutinous crew. The main problem was preserving food-stuffs. Food and water rapidly went bad when kept in barrels made of green wood, and could easily be spoilt if sea water, shipped during high seas, got to them. The ships were infested with rats which often ate the best food and spoilt much of the rest with their droppings; this is one of the reasons why a fine fat rat fetched such a high price on a long voyage; he had been better fed than the crew and was regarded as a delicacy. Ship's biscuit was full of weevils which had to be removed by expert tapping before a piece could be bitten off.

An eighteenth-century Admiral described ship's biscuit in vivid terms which were as true for the Age of Discoveries as they were for his own day:

It was so light that when you tapped it on the table it fell almost into dust and thereout numerous insects called weevils crawled; they were bitter to the taste and a sure indication that the biscuit had lost its nutritious particles: if, instead of these weevils large maggots with black heads made their appearance, then the biscuit was considered to be only in the first stage of decay; these maggots were fat and cold to the taste, but not bitter.

In times of real shortage, as on Magellan's voyage across the Pacific, anything that was remotely edible would be eaten, such as leather harness and wood shavings. Famine was always one of the most serious enemies of the sailor.

Here is a list of victuals taken by a seventeenth-century ship on a short voyage with a crew of 190 men:

8,000 lbs of salt beef.
2,800 lbs of salt pork.
A few beef tongues.
600 lbs of salt cod.
15,000 brown biscuits.
5,000 white biscuits.
30 bushels of oatmeal.
40 bushels of dried peas.
$1\frac{1}{2}$ bushels of mustard seed.
1 barrel of salt.
100 lbs of suet.
1 barrel of flour.
11 firkins (small wooden casks) of butter.
1 hogshead (a large cask) of vinegar.
10,500 gallons of beer.
3,500 gallons of water.
2 hogsheads of cider.

The basic ship's diet lacked not only variety but essential vitamins, so that deficiency diseases especially scurvy frequently attacked the crew and many would die unless fresh food could be obtained quickly.

There are horrifying descriptions of scurvy in the accounts of the voyages of Vasco da Gama, Magellan and Cartier. Some gifted captains like Sir John Hawkins avoided this danger by carrying large quantities of fruit and making frequent calls at port to obtain fresh supplies, but this was not always possible on long voyages in unknown waters. It was only in the seventeenth and eighteenth centuries that more and more captains took along stocks of lemon juice with them on long voyages to dose their men.

A poor, unbalanced diet threatened the crew's health and so did the unhygienic condition of the vessels and the men. The seamen were reluctant to wash either themselves or their ships; you must not imagine that the 'naos' were scrubbed and holystoned like the ships of the line in Nelson's day; they were often filthy and stinking. All kinds of rubbish was thrown through the scuppers or holes in the ship's side or overboard, but a great deal found its way down to the 'bilges' at the bottom of the ship where fairly large compost heaps could collect. The men's clothes and blankets and the very timbers of the ship were homes for lice, fleas, cockroaches and so on. But life on land was very little better in the fifteenth and sixteenth centuries especially in towns. One advantage that the sailors enjoyed compared with their cousins on land was the removal of sewage; the toilets were in the prow ('the heads') and the stern.

Boredom could be the greatest enemy of all. It has been said that a sailor's life consists of brief moments of violent action and danger and long, tedious periods of routine. The men on a good ship would find satisfaction in doing their work well as a Spanish writer points out:

When the master gives his orders, it is astonishing to see the industry and speed of the sailors in carrying them out. In a moment, some will be up the main crosstrees (the joining place of sections of the mast), some running up the ratlines holding onto the shrouds, some riding on the yards, some on the lower mast heads clinging to the caps or swarming up the topmasts and hanging from the trucks (wooden discs on the top of the masts through which flag halyards passed), some on deck hauling and gathering aft the sheets, and some climbing and swinging about in the rigging like monkeys in the trees.

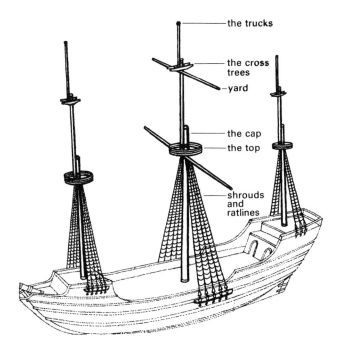

- the trucks
- the cross trees
- yard
- the cap
- the top
- shrouds and ratlines

A good captain would see that his crew had something to occupy them throughout the day whether it was practising some of the complicated manoeuvres involved in sailing, taking part in organised games, or dancing the hornpipe. When captains failed to do this, they suffered from the discontent and even mutiny of their crews; particularly, in summer time, there was too much time for idling, gambling, and getting on each other's nerves.

The punishment of wrongdoers was the responsibility of the Captain who usually dealt severely with them to impress the rest of the crew. Those who broke the rules were usually flogged with a cane or a whip. Lazy, mutinous and thieving seamen and those who fell asleep while on watch were strung up with ropes to the yardarm and then ducked in the sea, or as a contemporary put it:

violently let fall into the sea, sometimes twice, sometimes three times.

Other punishments included soaking with buckets of water, being tied to the mast with heavy weights hung around the neck till their back be ready to break, confinement in irons (iron hoops were driven into the deck over the criminal's legs), holding a marline spike* in the mouth, and fines.

In many ships there was a very strict code of behaviour and lists or ordinances were drawn up before the ship left port. The following extract is taken from the Ordinances drawn up by Sebastian Cabot for an intended voyage to Cathay:

VIII Item, that no blaspheming of God or detestable swearing be used in any ship, nor ribald, filthy or ungodly talk suffered in the company of any ship; neither carding, tabling nor other devilish games to be played whereby ensueth not only poverty to the players, but also strife, disagreements, brawling, fighting and sometimes murder to the utter destruction of the parties, provoking God's most just wrath and sword of vengeance. These and all such like pestilences to be punished at the discretion of the captain and master.

This may sound harsh and the work of a kill-joy, but Sebastian Cabot had sailed on long voyages himself and knew how these things could lead to trouble in the terribly over-crowded conditions on board ship.

* A pointed iron pin used to open the strands of rope for splicing.

Prompt payment of wages was another way in which a Captain could keep his men happy. A captured Spaniard reported admiringly of Sir Francis Drake:

I understood that all the men he carries with him receive wages, because when our ship was sacked no man dared to take anything without his orders. He shows them great favour, but punishes the least fault.

The practice of religion was another essential part of shipboard life which helped to remind the sailor of his duties. Many Captains were their own chaplains as well. Columbus led his men in singing the services and prevailed upon his men to swear to go on pilgrimages when they were in danger of being sunk. Some of the great Captains took their religious duties very seriously and saw themselves as missionaries spreading the Word amongst the heathen peoples they encountered; this is especially true of Magellan, Cortes, and Cartier.

Thus, to the problems of unknown seas and hostile inhabitants must be added famine, disease, boredom, and possible mutiny.

Questions to consider

1. What was a ship's 'Log'? Who had to keep it?
2. Which do you think were the best jobs on board ship? Which were the worst?
3. Why did these ships need such large crews?
4. Which essential foods tended to be missing from the diet provided for sailors on long ocean voyages?
5. What were the main causes of mutiny on board ship?
6. What measures did a good captain take to keep his men well disciplined and loyal?
7. What personal qualities do you think that a captain needed to be successful?

Suggestions for practical work

1. Imagine that you are a sailor in the sixteenth century; describe a voyage you have been on in the form of a diary, a ship's log or a play.
2. Make models of the sailors; the body can be made out of wire bound with bandage or strips of waste material, faces and hands, etc. can be made out of Playdoh; the dolls' clothes should be made out of materials as like those in use in the sixteenth century as possible. Alternatively, life-size flat representations of the sailor's body can be cut from cardboard or hardboard, and the clothes fitted on the frame; these clothes can be made of real material or coloured papers.
3. A mock-up of a seaman's trunk can be made. There should be an account explaining the need for each item included.
4. If you have the use of an oven, bake some ship's biscuit; if possible, produce a typical ship's meal of salt meat or fish, cheese or butter and ale.
5. The biscuit and other foods can be kept under similar conditions to those on board ship so that the speed and nature of their decay can be studied. (Consult your teacher and school cleaners before trying this.)

Suggestion for drama

Read the Spanish sailor's description of mealtime on page 55. Imagine the scene and act out a conversation between the crew when they had finished eating.

Drawings by Charles Sutton

6 Navigation

In the thirteenth century revolutionary changes took place in the science of navigation. Until that time sailors had depended upon their knowledge of the stars to steer their ships from one place to another.

First of all the magnetic compass was invented. From very early times, the lodestone, a natural magnetic stone, had been used both as a magical device to ward off evil spirits and as a means of discovering north—the Vikings carried them with them on their voyages to Iceland, Greenland, and probably America. The sea compass was a pivoted iron needle, magnetized by a lodestone, which gave the pilot of a ship a continuous sense of direction under overcast skies by day and night—in normal conditions, he was perfectly capable of steering by the stars at night. The compass is first mentioned in A.D. 1187 and was adapted for use at sea in about 1250. The sea compass enabled sailors to take compass bearings between different places with considerable accuracy so that charts could be constructed making this information available. One of the earliest references to the use of the compass is in Alexander Neckham's *De naturis rerum*.

When through cloudy weather hiding the sun in daytime or through the darkness of the night, mariners at sea lose their knowledge of the whereabouts of the quarter of the world to which they are sailing, they touch a needle with a magnet which turns round and stops with its point directed towards the north.

A German monk in the Middle Ages described a voyage he went on; here, he explains how the ship was guided through the sea:

And they have a compass near the mast and a second one on the topmost deck of the poop. And beside it all night long a lantern burns. There is always a man watching it and he never takes his eyes off it. He sings a sweet song telling that all goes well, and with the same chant directs the men at the tiller how to turn the rudder. Nor does the helmsman dare to move the tiller in the slightest degree except at the order of the one who watches the compass.

An illustration from a fifteenth-century French manuscript showing a sailor using a compass.

These early compasses had some weaknesses. On the one hand, they became 'exhausted' after a time and had to be 'refreshed' so that lodestones had to be taken on long voyages to re-magnetize the needle. But a far more serious weakness was compass variation which caused panic amongst Columbus's crew on his first voyage to the West Indies. The reasons for this were not understood until William Gilbert's work was published in 1600. William Gilbert was Queen Elizabeth I's court physician and had a deep interest in chemistry and physics. He suggested that the Earth itself was a great magnet having its north and south magnetic poles in the neighbourhood of the geographical poles and that the compass' magnetic needle turns to these as it does to those of a neighbouring magnet. The Earth had its own magnetic field with lines of force passing on continuously curved paths from regions in the southern hemisphere to regions in the northern hemisphere; the compass would follow these lines of force.

Although compass variation caused consternation, it did not prove to be a serious obstacle to navigation.

Secondly, means had to be discovered of working out the ship's position at sea. Latitude (the position north and south) was found by observing the altitude of the sun or pole-star with specially designed instruments, and longitude determined by dead reckoning.

Having obtained the altitude of the sun or pole-star, the navigator had to consult a 'nautical almanac' giving the positions of the sun and stars in the heavens each day, so that he could apply the necessary astronomical corrections to discover his exact latitude. Abraham Zacuto, a Moorish astronomer, prepared the nautical tables and instruments for Vasco da Gama's expedition in 1498, and his example was rapidly followed in Spain and the rest of Europe.

The discovery of Latitude was a relatively simple exercise compared to the calculation of Longitude, that is the position east or west of the ship's starting place. The early explorers had to rely on 'dead reckoning'. An hour's run was calculated with the aid of a sand glass and the navigator's accuracy depended almost entirely on his

A sixteenth-century compass rose

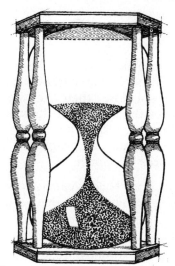

A sand glass

judgement. Even marking the passage of time was not easy as the sandglasses had to be promptly turned day and night, and the hours marked off on a slate with chalk or by putting pegs in a wooden board. Changes in the humidity of the air (the amount of water vapour present) affected the speed of the sand as did the pitching and rolling of the ship. Ariosto, the great Italian poet, described this primitive method:

One sailor on the poop and another at the prow, keeps the hourglass in front of him, and looks to see every half hour what distance has been covered and in what direction.

Another problem when calculating distance covered was changes of course. As a sailing ship cannot sail into the wind, it is often necessary for it to proceed to its destination by a series of zig-zag movements or 'tacks'. To solve the difficulty of recording changes of course, a traverse board was used and pegs put in the appropriate bearings.

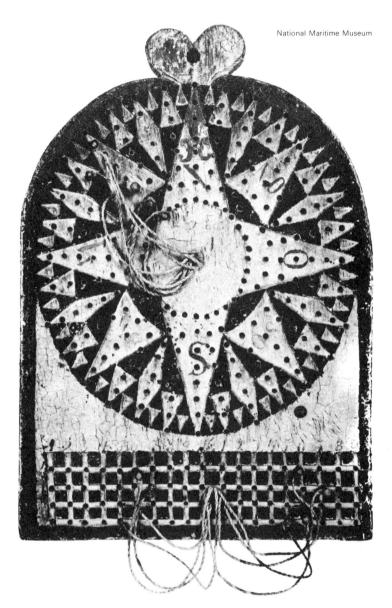

A traverse board: each peg represents half an hour's sailing

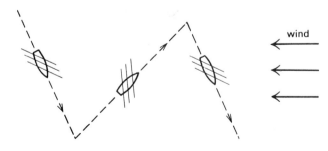

A ship tacking against the wind

wind

One of the favourite instruments used by the discoverers was the 'astrolabe' which was a simplified version of the astronomer's instrument. It was a circle of metal suspended from a ring with a movable arm or 'alidade' pinned in the centre; the outer rim of the circle was marked out in 360 degrees. The navigator held it in his left hand in the upright position and moved the alidade round until the sun shone directly through the two sights; the altitude was then read off the scale. Even if the astrolabe was hung from a special fitting, it was a difficult instrument to use in a pitching and rolling ship, so that navigators tried where possible to land and take 'shots' of the sun or stars. Both Columbus and Vasco da Gama used the astrolabe.

Another astronomical instrument that had been adapted for use at sea was the 'quadrant'. This consisted of a quarter-circle piece of metal, marked with a scale from 0° to 90° around the edge, with sights along the top edge to aim at a heavenly body. A plumb line hung from a hole at the top of the instrument and cut the scale enabling the pilot to read off the altitude. Diogo Gomes, one of Henry the Navigator's captains explained how he used the quadrant:

I had a quadrant when I went to these parts (the Guinea Coast). I marked on the scale of the quadrant the altitude of the Arctic Pole. I found it better than a chart: it is true that your course can be seen on the chart, but once you get wrong you cannot recover your true position.

The Portuguese captains usually marked the altitudes of each successive cape and river mouth upon their quadrant so that they could sail along the coastline of Africa with confidence on a later occasion.

A mariner's astrolabe

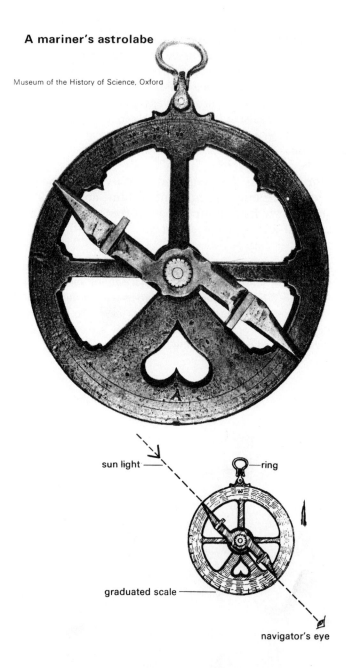

sun light — ring

graduated scale —

navigator's eye

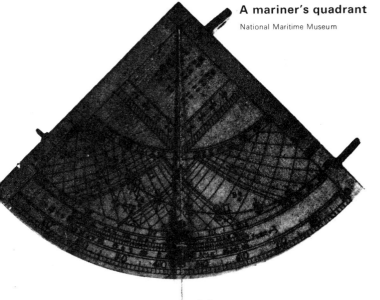

A mariner's quadrant

National Maritime Museum

The 'cross-staff' was also used to discover latitude and may have been copied from the instruments used by the Arabs. It is a pole marked out in degrees with one or more vertical crosspieces pierced with peep-holes at each end and another pair of peep-holes in a sight at the front of the pole. The observer held the staff out with the crosspiece almost vertical and moved the crosspiece up or down until the top peep-holes were lined up with the sun and the bottom ones with the horizon. This was an accurate and popular instrument as John Davis, the Elizabethan explorer, wrote:

No instrument can compare with the cross-staff for the use of seamen.

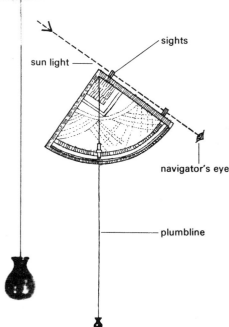

sights

sun light

navigator's eye

plumbline

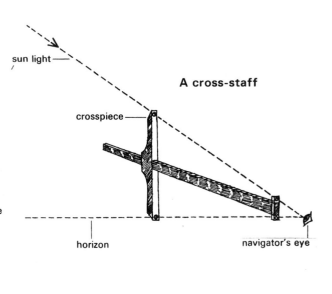

sun light

A cross-staff

crosspiece

horizon

navigator's eye

During the sixteenth century, the use of the 'log and line' helped the sailor to make a more accurate assessment of the ship's speed through the water. The first account of this method is to be found in William Bourne's *Regiment for the Sea*:

To know the ship's speed some do this, which is very good: they have a piece of wood and a line to throw overboard; in like manner they have a minute glass. The log or piece of wood is thrown out just as the sand starts to run; when the sand has run out, they haul in the log again and look to see how many fathoms the ship has gone in that time.

Of course for this method to work, the sailor had to make sure he heaved the log beyond the ship's wake and way. Later in 1624, Edmund Gunter suggested that knotted cords could be attached to the line at equal distances so that the sailor had only to count the number of knots paid out to obtain the ship's speed in miles per hour. This gave rise to the name 'knot' for nautical miles per hour.

Casting the log

Not all the explorers reached these scientific heights. Cadamosto, a captain in the employment of Henry the Navigator, did not use instruments but anchored at night and during the day hugged the coastline of Africa and constantly measured the depth of the water:

At dawn we made sail, always stationing one man aloft and two in the bows to watch for breakers, which would disclose the presence of shoals.

The 'Lead and Line' were used to measure the depth of the sea: the lead was a lump of metal which dragged the line to the seabed. It could be hollow and have tallow in its base for sticking to materials on the seabed; the 'core' was studied and its contents noted—expert mariners could often discover their whereabouts by their knowledge of the colour and nature of the deposits on the seafloor. The leadsman had to be a powerful individual because he would be required to heave the lead for long periods of time and he would have to be skilful as the lead and line were awkward to handle.

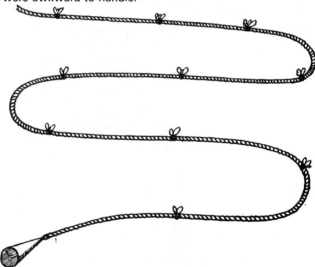

A lead and line. Each strip of cloth and leather represents a certain number of fathoms.

All these problems raised by the voyages of discovery led to research work and to the production of textbooks. Henry the Navigator is supposed to have founded a school for navigators at Sagres. King John of Portugal set up a study group to produce an improved method of finding the altitude of the sun and stars; this resulted in the publication of *the Regiment* (*the operating rules*) *of the Astrolabe and Quadrant* in 1509. Christopher Columbus appears to have known and used these early Portuguese manuals (the edition of 1509 is the first to have volumes surviving down to the present day). After the discovery of America, the Spanish took the lead and set up a school for pilots in the Casa de Contratacion or Board of Trade in Seville. The other European nations followed suit and William Bourne's *Regiment of the Sea* was such a manual.

Pigafetta, who was one of the survivors of Magellan's attempt to sail round the world, gave this advice to sailors:

If you wish to navigate to any place, you must first know its position, that is its longitude and latitude. Then, by means of the compass, you will point directly to the place. Since the compass varies to east and west, you must learn its variation and add or subtract that which is necessary, so that the ship's head regulated by the compass, may be pointed in the required direction.

Suggestions for practical work

1. Magnetize a steel needle and float it in a straw or on a piece of cork on water, and the needle will soon come to rest in the North-South line.
   OR Suspend the magnetized needle horizontally by its middle point with a fine thread and the North-South line will be indicated as before.
   A windrose can be made out of card and stuck underneath the needle to produce a fair likeness to an early medieval compass.

2. Model astrolabes, quadrants, and cross-staffs can be made out of wood and card, etc.
3. Large drawings can be made to illustrate the uses of the various instruments.
4. Pretend that you are a captain training members of the crew in navigation and write an account of the main points to be borne in mind.

Questions to consider

1. How did sailors steer their way through open seas in the days before there was a marine compass?
2. What did William Gilbert discover?
3. Why was the astrolabe difficult to use at sea?
4. What is meant by 'dead-reckoning'?
5. In what conditions did sandglasses prove to be unreliable?
6. How did the 'knot' get its name?
7. Why did sailing ships 'tack'?
8. What information did the use of the lead and line provide?
9. How did the sailors calculate the speed of their ships through the water?

Drawings by Charles Sutton

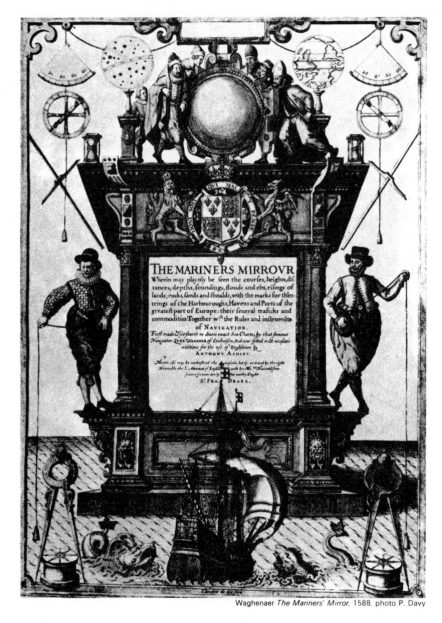

THE MARINERS MIRROVR
Wherin may playnly be seen the courses, heights, distances, depths, soundings, flouds and ebs, risings of lands, rocks, sands and shoalds, with the marks for then trings of the Harbouroughs, Havens and Ports of the greatest part of Europe: their seueral traficks and commodities Together with the Rules and instrumen̄s of NAVIGATION.
First made & set fourth in diuers exact Sea-Charts, by that famous Nauigater LVKE WAGHENAER of Enchuisen, And now fitted with necessari additions for the use of Englishmen by
ANTHONY ASHLEY.
Herein also may be understood the exploits latelj achiued by the right Honorable the L. Admiral of England with hir Ma. Nauie and some famous seruices don by the worthy Knight
Sr FRANCIS DRAKE.

Waghenaer *The Mariners' Mirror*, 1588. photo P. Davy

This is the title-page of an Elizabethan book on navigation. How many of the instruments shown in the picture can you name?

Explain what each instrument was used for.

What type of ship is shown? (See Chapter 3)

What evidence can you find that shows that this picture was made in the sixteenth century?

7 Cannons, Arms, and Armour

When the early explorers sailed in unknown seas, it was essential that they should be able to fight off any enemies. Even merchant ships carried cannon at this time to defend themselves against pirates and privateers. (Privateers were sailors who had a commission from a government allowing them to capture the shipping of a hostile nation.) The *Santa Maria*, Columbus' flagship, carried only one or two cannon, but this was unusual. Most of the famous explorers' ships carried enough guns to fire a broadside.

The earliest cannon were breech-loading and pointed through square ports fitted with heavy swinging port-lids; when a ship heeled over in strong winds, the sea could flood through open gun-ports and sink her—this happened to the *Mary Rose* in Henry VIII's reign; she sank with all hands off Spithead.

The cannon were usually mounted upon four wheeled wooden carriages which could be run in and out by means of rope tackles attached to the carriage and to ringbolts fastened to the deck and the bulwarks.

The breech loader was made in two parts: a 'breech' or powder chamber which could be lifted out of the gun carriage and a 'chase' or barrel which was clamped down to the carriage and reinforced with iron hoops. A wooden wedge fitted in behind the breech and took the shock of the recoil.

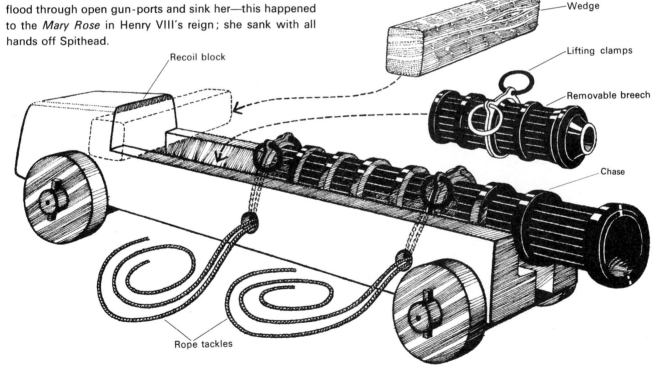

Recoil block

Rope tackles

Wedge

Lifting clamps

Removable breech

Chase

The breech was filled with gunpowder and replaced in its 'bed' in the guncarriage; it was held in place by some iron clamps. The wedge was forced down behind the breech. A cannonball was rammed down the chase and held in place by a wad. The gun was run out through the gun port, laid or aimed and fired by placing a lighted torch or linstock to the touch hole which was primed with gunpowder. The gunpowder in the breech exploded hurling the ball out of the barrel and the gun backwards—the recoil. The gun carriage ran back until the rope tackles became taut and stopped it; the ropes had to be kept in good order to prevent the guns from breaking loose and doing untold damage to the crew and the fabric of the ship.

After each discharge, the barrel had to be swabbed out with a wet sheepskin mop to cool it down and to remove any burning fragments that might remain from the discharge. If the barrel was too hot or smouldering materials were present, the new charge would ignite destroying the cannon and all those around it.

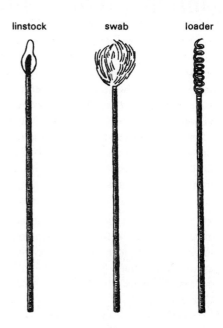

linstock swab loader

gun port

cannon balls

tackles breeching rope

Later, the muzzle-loader was introduced. It was a long metal tube closed at one end except for the touch hole and open at the other, the muzzle. The barrel seemed to taper towards the muzzle but inside the channel was the same width all the way down. The back part was made very thick so that it could withstand the shock of the explosion. On top, there were two 'dolphins' for lifting the gun out of its carriage. On each side, there was a 'trunnion' at the point of balance which fitted into hollows in the gun carriage.

This type of cannon had to be loaded in a different way: a cartridge, a canvas bag containing a measured amount of gunpowder, was pushed down the barrel; next, a cannon-ball was rammed down on top of it and wedged with a wad; the gunner primed the gun by thrusting a wire down the touch hole to pierce the cartridge and then filled the touch hole with some fine powder carried in a horn at his belt.

This kind of cannon could be raised or lowered because the barrel was balanced on top of the gun carriage. Each gun had a set of carefully graded wedges or 'quoins' which were inserted under the barrel to obtain the right elevation.

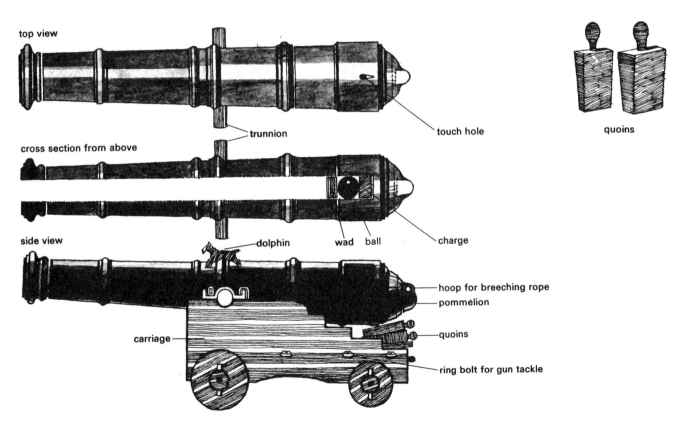

top view

cross section from above

side view

trunnion

touch hole

quoins

dolphin wad ball charge

hoop for breeching rope

pommelion

carriage

quoins

ring bolt for gun tackle

It would be pure luck if the first shot was anywhere near its target; usually the gunner would drop a few shots 'over' and 'short' before he found the range. Each cannon had individual qualities which had to be learnt by its crew; for example, every piece 'threw' to the left or the right and the gunner would have to allow for this when he trained the gun.

It was difficult for the gunners to keep up an accurate fire. If there was a little more powder in one charge than another the shot would be fired further. As the charges were weighed out in the semi-darkness of the powder room below water level, the weight of the charges did vary.

Cannonballs were not exactly uniform in size and shape, so their flight through the air varied in length and direction. As the barrel became hot, its fire became more and more inaccurate.

So cannon were most effective when a broadside (that is all the guns running down one side of the ship) was fired from point blank range into the enemy vessel.

cannon

During the sixteenth century, great developments took place in cannon manufacture and the 'great gun' was produced. Guns became divided into 'cannon' which were large callibre pieces (that is the diameter of the bore of the gun was large) capable of throwing a very heavy cannon-ball with great penetration over short distances, and 'culverins' which were very long barrelled, smaller calibre guns able to fire lighter balls over very long distances, with less penetration. This meant that if you wanted to sink your opponent, you had to go in close and pour broadside after broadside into his hull near or below the waterline, and be prepared to receive the same treatment. Alternatively you could stand off and pepper him from afar with your culverins hoping to disable him by shooting away spars and rigging before going in for the kill.

A cannon and a culverin

culverin

Stores of body armour consisting of 'back' and 'breast' plates and metal helms, often the famous morions, were carried on board ship. Leg armour was rarely worn at this time and lack of it was to prove to be Magellan's undoing and led to his death. Swords, daggers and halberds (combined spears and battleaxes) were used in hand to hand fighting by the officers and gentlemen while the ordinary sailors used any weapon they could lay their hands on. Hand guns were rapidly gaining in popularity and the arquebus was frequently mentioned and was used with great success by Cortes' men in Mexico. Crossbows and even longbows were still used.

Carrying their own cannon and arsenal of weapons, these little ships with their small crews were able to hold their own against the Arabs in the Indian Ocean and other hostile people (See Chapter 17 for an account of the Japanese reactions to *Pinto's* weapons.)

A morion

—halberd

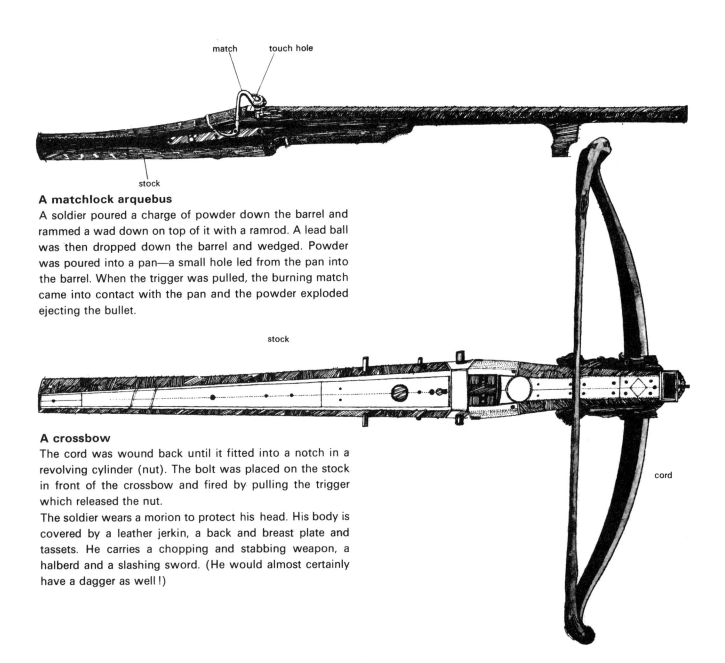

match   touch hole

stock

A matchlock arquebus

A soldier poured a charge of powder down the barrel and rammed a wad down on top of it with a ramrod. A lead ball was then dropped down the barrel and wedged. Powder was poured into a pan—a small hole led from the pan into the barrel. When the trigger was pulled, the burning match came into contact with the pan and the powder exploded ejecting the bullet.

stock

A crossbow

The cord was wound back until it fitted into a notch in a revolving cylinder (nut). The bolt was placed on the stock in front of the crossbow and fired by pulling the trigger which released the nut.

The soldier wears a morion to protect his head. His body is covered by a leather jerkin, a back and breast plate and tassets. He carries a chopping and stabbing weapon, a halberd and a slashing sword. (He would almost certainly have a dagger as well!)

cord

CANNONS, ARMS, AND ARMOUR | 73

Suggestions for practical work

1. Models of cannons can be made—there are commercially produced kits available. Sections through the body of the ship can be made showing how the guns were operated.
2. In the same way, small models can be made of the armour and weapons used. Full-size outlines of the human figure can be cut out of wood or stiff cardboard and clothed and armoured with a variety of materials including kitchen foil, cloth, leather, and even coloured papers.
3. The evolution of the cannon can be traced with appropriate drawings.
4. Friezes or detailed drawings and paintings can be made of battles described in the booklets, particularly those on Cortes and Magellan.
5. Imagine that you are on a sailing ship that is about to be attacked. Describe your preparations for battle.
6. Describe in words or pictures a battle between two galleons.

Questions to consider

1. Describe some of the jobs that gunners had to do.
2. Why were the gunports a danger to ships in heavy weather?
3. Why could some cannon fire further than others?
4. Why were cannon so erratic?
5. What were the main differences between 'cannon' and 'culverins'?
6. Why was it difficult to sink a wooden ship?
7. What other ways were there of defeating an enemy ship without sinking it?
8. Why were hand guns and crossbows so effective in sea fights? Where would their operators be stationed on board ship?
9. What weapons were used in hand-to-hand fighting?
10. What was the last resort of a ship faced by a more heavily armed opponent?

Drawings by Charles Sutton

8 Exploration of the West Coast of Africa

Henry the Navigator (1394–1460) was the third son of King John (1385–1433) of Portugal. For hundreds of years, the Portuguese had been fighting the Moslem Moors and when Prince Henry was 21, he fought with great distinction at the siege of Ceuta on the Moroccan coast. He saw that great wealth could be made from the Saharan trade in gold, ivory, pepper, and slaves. He realised that Portugal was too weak to conquer Morocco with its mountains and deserts, so he turned to the sea where the Portuguese had already proved themselves as merchant seamen.

He set up his headquarters at Sagres where he collected together the finest pilots, mapmakers, ship-designers, and scientists; these experts provided his sea captains with the information they needed as they set off each year to explore the unknown waters off the west coast of Africa. One day, Henry hoped to make contact with the mysterious Christian ruler Prester John so that they could join together to lead a crusade that would clear the Moslems from North Africa and the Holy Land.

Prince Henry was described in Azurara's Chronicles:

I say that this noble prince was of middle stature, a thickset man with large and powerful limbs, and bushy hair; his skin was white, but hard work and the battles of life altered its hue as time went on. His aspect, to those who beheld him for the first time, was severe; when anger carried him away his countenance became terrifying. He had force of mind and acute intelligence in a high degree. And you should note well that the spirit of this Prince was ever urging him both to begin and to carry out very great deeds. For which reason, after the taking of Ceuta in 1415, he always kept ships

Portrait of Henry the Navigator

Portuguese State Office

well armed against the Infidel (the Moslems) both for war, and because he had a wish to know about the land that lay beyond the isles of Canary and the Cape called Bojador; up to his time, neither by writings, nor by the memory of man was the nature of the land beyond that cape known with any certainty.

Some believed that St. Brendon had passed it; others said that two galleys had gone thither and had never returned. Prince Henry desired to know the truth of this; it seemed to him that if he or some other lord did not try to discover this no sailor or merchant would undertake this effort of his own accord; for it is very sure that they do not think to navigate anywhere but where they already know that they will find profit.

And seeing that no other prince was concerning himself in this matter, he sent his own ships to these countries in order to acquire knowledge in the service of God, and of the King Edward, his brother and lord, who was reigning at this time. And this was the first reason for his enterprise.

And the second was the thought that if in these territories there should be any population of Christians, or any harbours where men could enter without peril, they could bring to the realm many trade goods at little cost, as there would be no other person on these coasts who would trade with them; and that in like manner one could carry to these regions the merchandise of our realm, the sale of which would be of great profit to the natives.

The third reason was this: that it was said that the power of the Moors in this land of Africa was very much greater than was generally thought, and that there were among them neither Christians nor other races. And because every wise man is moved by desire to know the strength of his enemy, the Prince devised means to send his people in quest of information, in order to know the full extent of the Infidels' power.

The fourth reason was this: during one and thirty years of battles with the Moors the Prince had never found a Christian king or lord, outside this kingdom who, for the love of our Lord Jesus Christ, was willing to aid him in this war. He desired to know whether in those regions there might be any Christian princes in whom the charity and love of Christ were strong enough to cause them to aid him against these enemies of the faith.

The fifth reason was his great desire to increase the holy faith of Our Lord Jesus Christ by converting the peoples of Africa.

Prince Henry began to send his caravels along the west coast of Africa to find a way round Cape Bojador. The first voyages failed. A sailor wrote that:

Beyond this Cape there is no one, there is no population; the land is no less sandy than the deserts of Libya, where there is no water at all, neither trees nor green herbs. The sea is so shallow that at a league from the shore its depth is hardly a fathom. The tides are so strong that the ships which pass the Cape will never be able to return.

And at last after twelve years of effort, the Prince had a barque fitted out, appointing as the captain his squire, Gil Eannes, whom he afterwards knighted and rewarded largely . . . on this voyage, regardless of all peril he passed beyond the Cape, where he found matters very different from what he and others had imagined . . . they found lands without houses, but saw the footprints of men and camels.

Because of the siege of Tangier and the death of King Edward, there was a short pause in exploration from 1436 to 1441. Then another expedition led by Goncalves made a further advance.

However, after the departure of Antao Goncalves, he found his caravel to be in need of repair, so he caused it to be drawn up on shore, where it was cleaned and repaired while waiting for the tide, as though he had been in Lisbon harbour, a feat whose boldness provoked the admiration of his men. Then continuing their voyage, they went beyond Porto da Gale until they came to a Cape which they named Cape Blanco.

After some years of unspectacular progress, Prince Henry obtained the services of a twenty-one year old Venetian who has left a vivid record of his voyages and adventures:

Now I—Luigi Ca da Mosto—had sailed along nearly all the Mediterranean coasts, but, being caught by a storm off Cape St Vincent, had to take refuge in the Prince's town, and was there told of the glorious and boundless conquests of the Prince, which did exceedingly stir my soul—eager as it was for gain above all things else. My age, my vigour, my skill are equal to any toil; above all, my passionate desire to see the world and explore the unknown set me on fire with eagerness.

In 1455, Cadamosto sailed from Portugal for Madeira which was now 'thickly peopled with Portuguese'. From here, he sailed to the Canaries before reaching Cape Blanco where 'natives as black as moles were dressed in white flowing robes with turbans wound round their heads'. He pushed on for another four hundred miles and then sailed up the Senegal River for a further two hundred and fifty miles. He described the king and the people he found there:

You must know that this king is lord of a very poor people, and has no city in his country, but villages with huts of straw only . . . he has no regular income save that each year the lords of the country, in order to stand well with him, present him with horses, which are esteemed owing to their scarcity, forage, beasts such as cows and goats, vegetables, millet and the like. The King supports himself by raids which result in many slaves from his own as well as neighbouring countries. He employs these slaves in cultivating the land allotted to him, but he also sells many in return for horses and other goods.

You must know also that the men of these lands perform many women's tasks such as spinning, washing clothes and such things. The men and women are clean in their persons, since they wash themselves all over four or five times a day. These people dress thus: almost all constantly go naked, except for goatskins fashioned in the form of drawers. But the chiefs and those of standing wear a cotton garment. They have no ships; nor had they seen any from the beginning of the world until they saw those of the Portuguese.

A short time after Cadamosto's return, Diego Gomes set sail and explored the Gambia.

After passing a great river beyond Rio Grande we met such strong currents in the sea that no anchor would hold. The other captains and their men were much alarmed, and begged me to turn back. As the current grew even stronger we put back and came to a land, where there were groves of palms near the shore with their branches broken.

Then we found a plain covered with hay and more than five thousand animals like stags, but larger, who showed no fear of us. Five elephants with two young ones came out of a small river that was fringed with trees. We went back to the ships, and next day made our way from Cape Verde and saw the broad mouth of a great river, which we entered and guessed to be the Gambia. We went up the river as far as Cantor. Farther than this the ships could not go, because of the thick growth of trees and underwood. When the news spread through the country that the Christians were in Cantor, people came from Timbuktu in the North, from Mount Gelu in the South to see us. Here I was told there is gold in plenty, and caravans of camels go there with goods from Carthage, Tunis, Fez, Cairo, and all the lands of the Saracens. I asked the natives of Cantor about the road to the gold country. They told me the King lived in Kukia and was lord of all the mines on the right side of the river of Cantor, and that he had before the door of his palace a mass of gold just as it was taken from the earth, so large that twenty men could hardly move it, and that the King always fastened his horse to it. While I was thus trading with these negroes, my men became worn out with heat, and so we returned towards the ocean.

Gomes did not forget that it was his duty to try and convert the Africans, and was presented with a marvellous opportunity on his return voyage.

. . . while I stayed here (at the mouth of the Gambia) three days, I learned all the mischief that had been done to the Christians by a certain King. So I took pains to make peace with him and sent him many presents by his own men in his own

This picture of Fort Elmina is an illustration from a book built the first fort there.

canoes. Now the King was in great fear of the Christians, lest they should take vengeance upon him. When the King heard that I always treated the natives kindly, he came to the riverside with a

ished in 1670—nearly two hundred years after the Portuguese

great force, and, sitting down on the bank, sent for me. And so I went and paid him all respect. There was a Bishop of his own faith, who asked me about the God of the Christians, and I answered him as God had given me to know. At last the King was so pleased with what I said that he sprang to his feet and ordered the Mohammedan Bishop to leave his country within three days.

When Gomes returned home in 1458, Prince Henry followed up this triumph by sending a priest and a member of his own household to the King. This was almost his last success as in 1460 Prince Henry died.

His nephew, Alphonso V (1438–81), was too busy with matters of state to supervise the further exploration of the coast so he granted a lease to Fernao Gomes, a Lisbon merchant. He was given the sole right to trade with West Africa and in return he paid the king 200,000 *reis* a year. In addition, he promised that his seamen would explore at least 500 leagues of new coast each year. The Gulf of Guinea was explored and his sailing masters discovered that the coast carried on southwards to the equator and beyond. Their most important discovery was the great gold market in what became known as the Gold Coast.

On the death of Alphonso, his son John II (1481–95) took over control of the trade and had a fort called Elmina built to guard Portuguese interests.

... he ordered the equipping of a fleet of ten caravels and two urcas (hulks) to carry hewed stones, tiles and wood, as well as munitions and provisions for six hundred men, one hundred of whom were craftsmen and five hundred soldiers. Diogo de Azambuja was captain major of these ships ... the chief merchant was told to take a double supply of cloths, bracelets, basins and other things he had ordered to be presented to the King and his chiefs as was customary. The work progressed so rapidly that in 20 days the outer wall of the castle was raised to a good height, and the tower to the first floor.

EXPLORATION OF THE WEST COAST OF AFRICA | 79

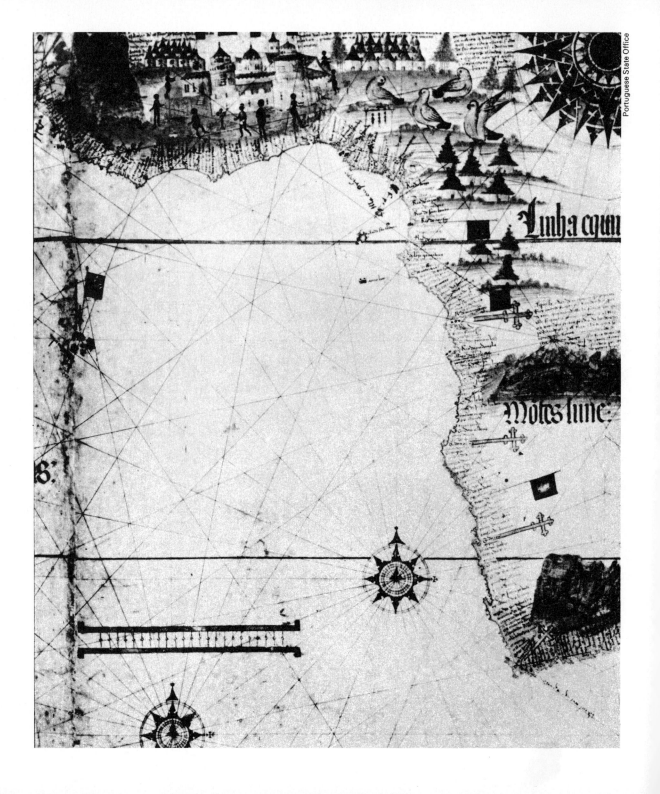

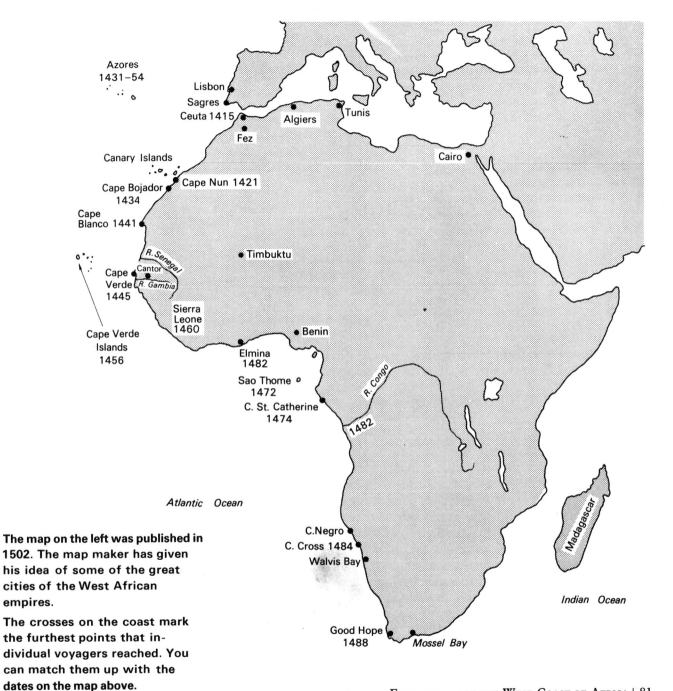

Azores
1431–54

Lisbon
Sagres
Ceuta 1415
Algiers
Fez
Tunis
Cairo

Canary Islands

Cape Bojador
1434
Cape Nun 1421

Cape
Blanco 1441

R. Senegal

Timbuktu

Cape
Verde
1445
Cantor
R. Gambia

Cape Verde
Islands
1456

Sierra
Leone
1460

Benin

Elmina
1482

Sao Thome
1472

C. St. Catherine
1474

R. Congo

1482

Atlantic Ocean

Madagascar

C.Negro
C. Cross 1484
Walvis Bay

Indian Ocean

Good Hope
1488
Mossel Bay

The map on the left was published in 1502. The map maker has given his idea of some of the great cities of the West African empires.

The crosses on the coast mark the furthest points that individual voyagers reached. You can match them up with the dates on the map above.

When the fort was built and the Portuguese were able to control the export of gold from Elmina, John II heard more exciting news from Africa.

Among the many things which King John learnt from the ambassador of the King of Benin . . . was that to the East of Benin at 20 moons' journey there lived the most powerful monarch of these parts, who was called Ogané. Wherefore the King and his cosmographers, taking into consideration Ptolemy's general map of Africa concluded that he must be Prester John. And it also appeared to King John that if his ships continued along the coast they had discovered, they could not fail to reach the land where the promontory Praso (Ptolemy's Prasum Promont) was the limit of the country. Therefore taking into consideration all these facts which increased his ardour for the plan of discovering India, he determined to send immediately in the year 1486 both ships by sea and men by land, in order to get to the root of this matter which inspired so much hope in him.

There is no contemporary account of the voyage of Bartholomew Dias, but a most interesting note has been discovered in what has thought to be Christopher Columbus' handwriting in his copy of *Imago Mundi*, a geography book by Pierre d'Ailly.

Note, that in December of this year, 1486, there landed at Lisbon Bartholomew Dias, the commander of three caravels, whom the King of Portugal had sent to Guinea to explore the land and who reported that he had sailed 600 leagues beyond the furthest point reached hitherto, that is 450 leagues to the South and then 150 leagues to the North, as far as the Cape of Good Hope, its latitude, as determined by the astrolabe, being 45° South (in fact nearer 35°S) and its distance from Lisbon 3100 leagues. This voyage he had depicted and described from league to league upon a chart, so that he might show it to the king; at all of which I was present.

Adapted from

1. *The Conquests and Discoveries of Henry the Navigator*, edited and translated by Bernard Miall (George Allen and Unwin Ltd.).
2. *The Discovery and Conquest of Guinea by Gomez Eannes de Azurara*, edited and translated by R. Beazley and E. Prestage (Hackluyt Society).
3. *The Voyages of Cadamosto*, edited and translated by G. R. Crone (Hakluyt Society).
4. E. G. Ravenstein, The Voyages of Diogo Cao and Bartholomew Dias, *The Journal of the Royal Geographical Society* (Dec. 1900).

Questions to consider

What did Henry the Navigator hope that his sailors would find in Africa?

What did the sailors fear?

What discoveries in Senegal do you think surprised the Portuguese sailors?

What did the Portuguese do in Gambia? What did they find there?

Why did the Portuguese build Fort Elmina?

What news pleased King John II most? Why was he so pleased?

Why do you think Columbus was so interested in Dias' voyage?

9 Vasco da Gama's Voyage to India

These extracts were taken from the journal kept by an unknown crew member of the *Sao Rafael*, one of da Gama's fleet.

In the year 1497, King Dom Manuel, the first of that name in Portugal, dispatched four vessels to make discoveries and go in search of spices. Vasco da Gama was the captain-major of these vessels: the *S. Gabriel* (flagship), the *S. Rafael* (Paulo da Gama), the *Berrio* (Nicolau Coelho) and the *Goncalo Nunes* (a store ship).

He sailed from Lisbon in July, passed between the Canary Islands and the coast, and ran before the north-east trade winds:

We arrived at the island of Santiago (the largest of the Cape Verde Islands) and joyfully anchored in the Bay of Santa Maria, where we took on board meat, water, and wood, and did the much needed repairs to our yards.

On Thursday, 3rd August, we left in an easterly direction.

Abreast of Sierra Leone, they turned and sailed far to the west before swinging back on to the route to the south.

On Wednesday, 1st November, the day of All Saints, we perceived many indications of the neighbourhood of land including gulf weed which grows along the coast.

On Saturday, the 4th of the same month, a couple of hours before break of day, we made soundings in 110 fathoms (a Portuguese fathom is 5 feet, 10 inches), and at nine o'clock we sighted the island of St. Helena. We then drew near to each other, and having put on our gala clothes, we saluted the captain-major by firing our bombards, and dressed the ships with flags and standards.

At daybreak on **Thursday, 16th November,** having careened (see page 49) our ships and taken in wood, we set sail. At that time we did not know how far we might be below the Cape of Good Hope. We therefore stood out towards the south-south-west, and late on Saturday we beheld the Cape.

They tried to sail round the Cape several times.

On Sunday morning, 19th November, we once more made for the Cape, but were unable to round it, for the wind was from the south-south-west, whilst the Cape juts out towards the south-west. At last, on Wednesday, at noon, having the wind astern, we succeeded in doubling the Cape and then ran along the coast. Late on Saturday, 25th November, the day of St. Catherine, we entered the bay of Sao Bras (thought to be Mossel Bay) where we remained for thirteen days.

During the following days, they sailed along the coast in spite of difficulties.

. . . we sailed along the coast before a stern-wind, and when the wind swung round to the east we stood out to sea. And thus we kept making tacks (see page 61) until sunset on Tuesday, when the wind again veered to the west. We then lay to during the night in order that we might on the following day examine the coast and find out where we were.

In the morning we made straight for the land and at ten o'clock found ourselves once more at Cross Island that is 60 leagues behind our dead reckoning. This was due to the currents, which are very strong here.

That very day we again went forward by the route we had already attempted, and being favoured during three or four days by a strong stern-wind, we were able to overcome the currents which we had feared might frustrate our plans. Henceforth it pleased God in His mercy to allow us to make headway.

By Christmas Day, we had discovered seventy leagues of coast (beyond Dias' furthest landfall). On that day, after dinner, when setting a studding sail (an extra piece of canvas attached to the mainsail) we discovered that the mast had sprung a couple of yards below the top and that the crack opened and shut. We lashed it together with back-stays (ropes), hoping to be able to repair it thoroughly as soon as we should reach a sheltered port.

The fleet continued to leap-frog up the east coast of Africa, stopping every so often.

Continuing our course we perceived the broad mouth of a river (the Kiliman River). As it was necessary to find out where we were, we entered. The country is low and marshy, and covered with tall trees yielding an abundance of various fruits, which the inhabitants eat. These people are black and well made. They go naked, merely wearing a piece of cotton stuff around their loins, that worn by the women being larger than that worn by the men. The young women are good-looking. Their lips are pierced in three places, and they wear in them bits of twisted tin. These people took much delight in us. As to ourselves, we spent thirty-two days in the river (24th January to 24th February), careening the ships, and repairing the mast of the *Rafael*.

They paid a visit to Mozambique.

The captain thought that we should enter this bay in order that we might find out what sort of people we had to deal with; that Nicolau Coelho should go first in his vessel, to take soundings at the entrance, and that, if found practicable, we should follow him. As Coelho prepared to enter he struck the point of the island and broke his helm, but disengaged himself and regained deep water. I was with him at the time. When we were again in deep water we struck our sails and cast anchor at a distance of two bowshots from the village.

The people of this country are of ruddy complexion and well made. They are Mohammedans (Moslems), and their language is the same as that of the Moors (Arabic). Their dresses are of fine linen or cotton stuffs, with variously coloured stripes, and of rich and elaborate workmanship. They wear toucas (caps) with borders of silk embroidered in gold. They are merchants, and trade with white Moors, four of whose vessels were at the time in port, laden with gold, silver, cloves, pepper, ginger, and silver rings, as also with quantities of pearls, jewels, and rubies, all of which articles are used by the people of this country.

We were told, moreover, that Prester John resided not far from this place, and that the inhabitants of these cities were great merchants and owned big ships. The residence of Prester John was said to be far in the interior, and could only be reached on camels.

On Saturday, 7th April, we cast anchor off Mombasa, but did not enter the port. No sooner had

British Museum

Diogo Homen's map, 1558. The details of Prester John and the elephant above are enlarged from it

Portrait of Vasco da Gama

Museu Nacional de Arte Antiga, Lisbon

we been sighted than a dhow manned by Moors (Arabs), came out to us; in front of the city there lay numerous vessels all decked out in flags. And, we, anxious not to be outdone, also dressed our ships. At midnight there approached us a dhow with about a hundred men, all armed with cutlasses and bucklers (shields). When they reached the captain-major's vessel they attempted to board her, but only four or five of the most distinguished men among them were allowed on board.

Azores

Lisbon

Canary Islands

Cape Bojador

Cape Verde Islands

Cape Verde

R. Congo

Mo

Good Hope

→ Vasco Da Gama's Voyage to India 1497

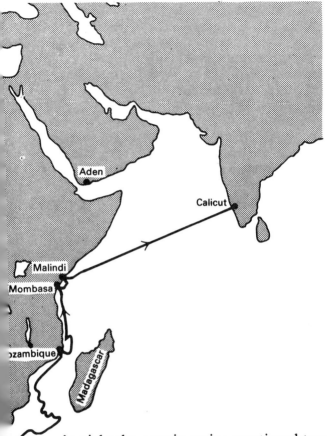

cable. The men on watch thought at first that they were tunny fish, but when they realised their mistake they shouted to the other vessels. The other swimmers had already got hold of the rigging of the mizzen-mast. Seeing themselves discovered, they silently slipped down and fled.

After the malice and treachery planned by these dogs had been discovered, we still remained on Wednesday and Thursday . . .

The fleet sailed north to Malindi where Arab/Portuguese relations were strained and da Gama had to take a firm line to obtain supplies and a pilot.

On the following Sunday, 22nd April, the king of Malindi's dhow brought on board one of his confidential servants, and as two days had passed without any visitors, the captain-major had this man seized and sent word to the king that he required the pilots whom he had promised. The king, when he received this message, sent a 'Christian'* pilot (a Hindu from Gujarat in India called Ahmed ibn Majid) and the captain-major allowed the gentleman, whom he had retained in his vessel to go away.

We left Malindi on Tuesday, the 24th of the month, for a city called Calicut . . .

On the following Sunday, we once more saw the north star, which we had not seen for a long time.

They crossed the Indian Ocean.

On Friday, 18th May, after having seen no land for 23 days we sighted lofty mountains, and having all this time sailed before the wind we could not have made less than 600 leagues. That night we

* da Gama thought that the Hindus were Christians because of some similarities in worship.

At night the captain-major questioned two Moors whom we had on board, by dropping boiling oil upon their skin, so that they might confess any treachery intended against us. They admitted that orders had been given to capture us as soon as we entered the port.

About midnight, two ships, with many men in them, approached. The ships stood off whilst the men entered the water, some swimming in the direction of the *Berrio*, others in that of the *Rafael*. Those who swam to the *Berrio* began to cut her anchored two leagues from the city of Calicut, and we did so because our pilot mistook Capia, a town at that place, for Calicut.

The city of Calicut is inhabited by 'Christians'. They are of tawny complexion. Some of them have big beards and long hair, whilst others clip their hair short or shave the head, merely allowing a tuft to remain on the crown as a sign that they are Christians (Hindus). They also wear moustaches. They pierce their ears and wear much gold in them. They go naked down to the waist, covering their lower extremities with fine cotton stuffs. But it is only the most respectable who do this, for the others manage as best they are able.

When we arrived the king was fifteen leagues away. The captain-major sent two men to him with a message, informing him that an ambassador had arrived from the king of Portugal with letters, and that if he desired it, he would take them where the king then was.

The king presented the bearers of this message with much fine cloth. On the following morning, which was **Monday, 28th May,** the captain-major set out to speak to the king. The king was in a small court, reclining upon a couch covered with a cloth of green velvet. The captain, on entering, saluted in the manner of the country: by putting his hands together, then raising them towards Heaven . . . he (the king) invited him to address himself to the courtiers present. The captain-major replied that he was the ambassador of the king of Portugal and the bearer of a message, which he could only deliver to him personally. In reply to this (message) the king said that he was welcome, that for his part, he regarded him as a friend and brother, and would send ambassadors with him to Portugal.

On Wednesday morning the Moors returned, and took the captain to the palace. The palace was crowded with armed men. Our captain was kept waiting with his conductors for fully four long hours outside a door. When he entered, the king said that he had expected him on Tuesday. The captain said that the long road had tired him, and that for this reason he had not come to see him. The king replied that he had told him that he came from a very rich kingdom, and yet had brought him nothing. The king then asked him what he had come to discover: precious stones or men?

After this very unsatisfactory meeting with the king, da Gama was prevented from returning to his ship for some days but his courage and that of the crews brought about a change of policy and he was released. The Portuguese were able to sell their merchandise and buy a quantity of pepper and cinnamon. The King of Calicut gave the captain-major a letter to his own king:

'Vasco da Gama, a gentleman of your houshold, came to my country, whereat I was pleased. My country is rich in cinnamon, cloves, ginger, pepper, and precious stones. That which I ask of you in exchange is gold, silver, corals, and scarlet cloth'.

On Wednesday, 29th (of August), the captain-major and the other captains agreed that, as we had discovered the country we had come in search of, as well as spices and precious stones, and since it appeared impossible to establish cordial relations with the people, it would be as well to make our departure. And it was resolved that we should take with us the Indians whom we had detained, as, on our return to Calicut, they might be useful to us in establishing friendly relations. We therefore set sail and left for Portugal, greatly rejoicing at our good fortune in having made so great a discovery.

Owing to frequent calms and foul winds it took us three months less three days to cross this gulf, the Indian Ocean (5th October to 2nd January, 1499), and all our people again suffered from their gums, which grew over their teeth, so that they could not eat. Their legs and other parts of the body also swelled and these swellings spread until the sufferer died, without exhibiting symptoms of any other disease. Thirty of our men died in this manner— an equal number having died previously—and those able to navigate each ship were only seven or eight, and even these were not as well as they ought to have been. We had come to such a pass that all bonds of discipline had gone. Whilst suffering this affliction we addressed vows and petitions to the saints on behalf of our ships. The captains held council, and they agreed that if a favourable wind enabled us we would return to India whence we had come. But it pleased God in his mercy to send us a wind which in the course of six days carried us within sight of land.

Shortly after the last extract, the manuscript comes to an abrupt end. We know from other sources that da Gama reached Lisbon in September 1499, and, although he had lost two of his ships and almost half his men, the trip showed a profit of 6,000 per cent.

And the king, overjoyed at his coming, sent a nobleman and several gentlemen to bring him to court; where, being arrived through crowds of spectators, he was received with extraordinary honour. For this glorious service, the privilege of being called Don was given to his family: to his Coat of Arms was added part of the king's. He had a pension of three thousand ducats yearly, and he

De Bry, Voyages, c 1600. National Maritime Museum

This is part of an engraving of Lisbon harbour, about a hundred years after da Gama's journey.

was afterwards presented to greater honours for his services in the Indies.

King Manuel of Portugal wrote a letter to the King and Queen of Castile in July 1499:

And Your Highnesses may believe in accordance with what we have learnt concerning the Christian people whom these explorers reached, that it will be possible to do much in the service of God and the exaltation of the Holy Faith once they shall have been converted and fully fortified in it. And when they have been fortified in the faith there will be an opportunity for destroying the Moors in those parts. Moreover we hope the spice trade shall be diverted to the natives and ships of our own kingdom so that henceforth all Christendom shall be able to provide itself with these spices and precious stones.

Adapted from *A Journal of the first Voyage of Vasco da Gama*, edited and translated by Ernst George Ravenstein (Hakluyt Soc., 1898).

Questions to consider

What did the Portuguese sailors learn about the people who lived on the east coast of Africa?

What were da Gama and his crew looking for in India? Did they find what they expected?

Was the voyage a success?

What was the most difficult part of the voyage for the navigators?

Which was the most uncomfortable and dangerous time for the sailors?

Pretend that you were present at the first meeting of the King of Calicut and Vasco da Gama (the captain-major). Describe in words or pictures what you saw.

How did the King of Calicut treat the Portuguese?

10 The First Voyage of Christopher Columbus

Museo Navale, Genoa

Christopher Columbus

Christopher Columbus was born in or near the Italian port of Genoa between 1450 and 1452. His father was a successful weaver and seller of textiles. Christopher became a seaman and claimed that he had sailed on all the main European trade routes. He studied astronomy, geography, and mathematics and came to the conclusion that China could be reached by sailing directly across the Atlantic Ocean. For some years, he and his brother visited the courts of kings of Europe trying to persuade one of them to finance an expedition. Finally he managed to win the support of Ferdinand of Aragon and Isabella of Castille.

The extracts that follow come from Columbus' letters and from the official journal of the voyage—the log book. This log was compiled by Bartolomew Las Casas from Columbus' own journal which has been lost. The narrative is Las Casas' but from time to time he quotes Columbus' own words.

Columbus wrote:

I left the city of Granada on the 12th day of May, in the year 1492, and came to the town of Palos, which is a seaport, where I equipped three vessels well suited for such service (the *Santa Maria* of 100 tons, the *Nina* of 60 tons, and the *Pinta* of about 40 tons), and departed from that port well supplied with provisions and with many sailors on the 3rd day of August of the same year, being Friday, half an hour before sunrise, taking the route to the Canary Islands . . .

Throughout the voyage, Columbus had trouble with his crews and the inferior materials used in the construction of his caravels; the writer of the journal reported:

Monday, 6th August The rudder of the caravel *Pinta* became unhinged and Martin Alonzo Pinzon, who was in command, believed or suspected that it was by contrivance of Gomes Rascon and Cristobal Quintero, to whom the caravel belonged, for they dreaded to go on this voyage. The Admiral says that before they sailed these men had been grumbling and making difficulties.

The Admiral was much disturbed at not being able to help the *Pinta* without danger, and he says that he was eased of some anxiety when he reflected that Martin Alonzo Pinzon was a man of energy and ingenuity.

Afterwards the Admiral took her to the Canary Islands.

Between 10th-31st August they repaired the *Pinta* thoroughly ... they fitted the *Pinta* with square sails for she was lateen rigged. It is said that the *Nina* was rerigged at the same time.

Thursday, 6th September Having taken on water, wood and meat, he finally made sail from the island of Gomara. The Admiral learned that there were three Portuguese caravels cruising about looking for him—this must have been because the King of Portugal was angry that the Admiral should have served the King and Queen of Spain.

On the outward journey they enjoyed good weather but Columbus expected trouble with the crew and took precautions.

Sunday, 9th September This day the Admiral calculated that we had run 19 leagues but he decided to record less than this number so that the crew would not be terrified and disheartened if the voyage was of long duration.

Sunday, 16th September The Admiral says that on the day and ever afterwards, they met with temperate breezes so that there was great pleasure in enjoying the mornings, which only lacked the song of the nightingales. He says that the weather was like April in Andalusia.

According to Herrera, a member of the crew, for 11 days, they did not even have to trim the sails. But then the wind changed and blew from the west. Columbus wrote:

Saturday, 22nd September This head wind was very necessary for me, because my people were much alarmed at the thought that in these seas no wind ever blew in the direction of Spain.

The writer of the journal reported:

Wednesday, 10th October Here the people could bear no more. They complained of the length of the voyage. But the Admiral cheered them up in the best way he could giving them high hopes of the advantages they might gain. He added that, however much they might complain, he had to go to the Indies, and that he would go on until he found them with the help of our Lord.

Thursday, 11th October The crew of the caravel *Nina* saw signs of land, and a small branch covered with berries. Everyone breathed afresh and rejoiced at these signs. The land was first seen by a sailor named Rodrigo de Triana.

Friday, 12th October The vessels were hove to, waiting for daylight. They arrived at a small island called in the language of the Indians, Guanahani (San Salvador or today, Watling Island). Presently they saw naked people. The Admiral went on shore in the armed boat, with Martin Alonzo Pinzon, and Vicente Yanez, the captain of the *Nina*. The Admiral took the royal standard. Having landed, they saw very green trees, and many streams of water, and fruits of many kinds. The Admiral called to the others that they should bear faithful witness that he, in the presence of all, had taken possession of the island for the King and for the Queen.

Here follow the actual words of the Admiral: 'They appeared to me to be a race of very poor people. They go as naked as when their mothers

De Bry *Voyages* c.1600. Bodleian Library

Columbus landing on Watling Island in 1492—an engraving made about 100 years later

Are the details in this picture correct? Look at the costumes and at the ships. If you can, compare them with pictures of fifteenth-century costume and ships. Did the islanders really have such elaborate metal objects?

bore them even the women. All whom I saw were youths, none more than 30 years of age. They are very well made with handsome bodies, and very good faces. Their hair is short and coarse, almost like the hair of a horse's tail. They paint themselves black but are the colour of the Canary Islanders neither black nor white. They neither carry nor know anything of weapons, for I showed them swords, and they cut themselves through ignorance. They would make good, intelligent servants, for I observed that they quickly took in what was said to them, and I believe that they could easily become Christians as they appear to have no religion.

In these islands, I have not found any human monsters as many expected; on the contrary, among all these people, good looks are highly valued. They are not Negroes, as in Guinea but have flowing hair; they are not born where the force of the sun's rays is excessive. In these islands where there are high mountains, the winter is bitterly cold but they endure it through habit and with the help of food mixed with many and excessively hot spices. Thus I have found no monsters.' These are the words of the Admiral.

After visiting several small islands, Columbus reached Cuba on 28 October and spent 12 days exploring the coast and trying to make contact with the local rulers. Columbus described what happened in a letter written on his return to Spain:

When I reached Cuba I followed its coast to the westward, and because it was so extensive I thought it must be the mainland of China. Since there were neither towns nor villages on the sea-shore, but only hamlets where people fled immediately, I continued on the same course thinking that I could not fail to find great cities and towns. At the end of many leagues, I saw that there was no change except that the coast was bearing northwards, which I wished to avoid, since winter was already beginning. I retraced my path as far as a certain harbour (Puerto Gibara) known to me. And from that point; I sent two men inland to learn if there were a king or great cities. They travelled for three days and found an infinite number of small hamlets and people without number, but nothing of importance.

He was disappointed at not making contact with the Great Khan of China but wrote a very favourable description of his discoveries.

Without doubt, there is in these lands a vast quantity of gold, and the Indians I have on board do not speak without reason when they say that in these islands there are places where they dig up gold, and wear it on their necks, ears, arms, legs; the rings are very large. There are also precious stones, pearls, and an infinity of spices. . . . There is also a great quantity of cotton and I believe it would sell well here in the cities of the Great Khan (which will be discovered without doubt) without sending it to Spain.

Continuing his voyage through the West Indies the Admiral found it increasingly difficult to control his men. The writer of the log book reports:

Wednesday, 21st November This day Martin Alonzo Pinzon went off with the caravel *Pinta* in disobedience to and against the wish of the Admiral and out of greed thinking that an Indian who had been put on board could show him where there was much gold. So he parted company, not owing to bad weather, but because he so chose.

After the *Pinta*'s desertion trading expeditions were sent out; here is one example

. . . the Admiral sent six men to a large village, because the Chief had come the day before and said that he had some pieces of gold. When the Christians arrived, the Secretary of the Admiral took the Chief by the hand. The Admiral had sent him to prevent the others from cheating the Indians. As the Indians are so simple, and the Spanish so avaricious and grasping, they are not satisfied that the Indians should give them all

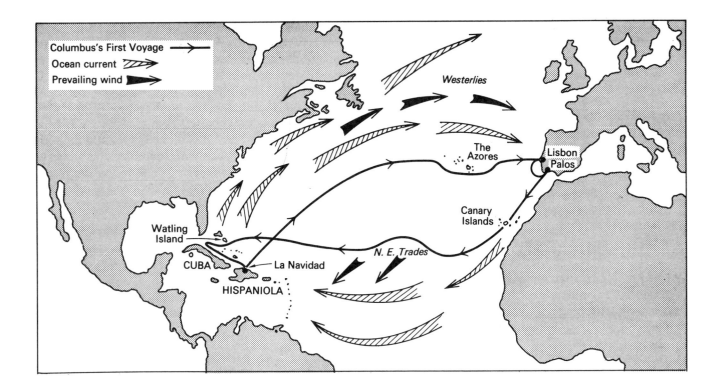

Columbus's First Voyage →
Ocean current
Prevailing wind

Westerlies

The Azores

Lisbon
Palos

Canary Islands

Watling Island

CUBA — La Navidad

HISPANIOLA

N. E. Trades

they want in exchange for a bead or a bit of glass, but the Spanish would take everything without any return at all. The Admiral always forbids this, although with the exception of gold, the things given by the Indians are of little value.

Tuesday, 25th December As it was calm, the sailor who steered the ship (the *Santa Maria*) thought he would go to sleep, leaving the tiller in charge of a boy. It pleased our Lord that at 12 o'clock at night, when the Admiral had retired to rest, and all had fallen asleep, seeing that it was a dead calm and the sea like glass, the current carried the ship onto one of the sandbanks (actually a coral reef). The Admiral at once rushed up on deck and presently, the master of the ship, whose watch it was, came up. The Admiral ordered him and others to launch the boat to run an anchor out astern but they tried to take refuge in the caravel (the *Nina*). The caravel's crew would not let them on board, and they therefore returned to the ship. When the Admiral saw that his own people fled in this way, he ordered the masts to be cut down and the ship to be lightened as much as possible to see if she would come off. But as the water continued to rise, nothing more could be done. Then the timbers opened and the ship was lost.

Columbus abandoned the *Santa Maria* and transferred his crew to the *Nina*. On reaching the island of Hispaniola, he decided that the time had come to construct a permanent base. On his return to Spain he wrote to Ferdinand and Isabella:

I have taken possession of a large town on the island of Hispaniola to which I have given the name Villa de Navidad (Christmas Town) and in it I have built a fort. Its situation is most convenient as it is well placed for the gold mines and for taking part in the trading of this island as well as that of the mainland belonging to the Great Khan.

The Journal states that:

Friday, 4th January 1493 He left on that island of Hispaniola, 39 men in the fortress and says that they were great friends of the Guacanageri (the Indians). . . . He left behind all the merchandise which had been provided for bartering, which was a lot so that they could trade for gold. He also left a year's supply of bread, wines and much artillery as well as the ship's boat so that they, most of them being sailors, might go, when it was convenient, to search for the gold mine. They were also to find a good site for a town, for this was not a desirable port. He also left seeds for sowing, and his officers, the Alquazil and Secretary, as well as a ship's carpenter, a caulker, a good gunner well acquainted with artillery, a cooper, a physician and a tailor, all being seamen as well.

Sunday, 6th January, The Admiral ordered a sailor to go to the masthead to look out for reefs, and he saw the caravel *Pinta* coming, with the wind aft. When she joined the Admiral, Martin Alonzo Pinzon came on board the caravel *Nina* and excused himself by saying that he had parted company with the Admiral against his will. . . .

R. A. Skelten, *History of Cartography*, C. A. Watts & Co Ltd, 1964

A sketch map of Hispaniola drawn by Columbus. (Hispaniola today is Haiti and the Domican Republic.)

Columbus decided to return home as quickly as possible to get rid of such an evil company with whom he thought it necessary to dissemble, although they were a mutinous set . . . for it was not a fitting time to deal out punishment.

The return 'leg' of the journey was harder than the voyage to the Indies:

Monday, 14th February This night the wind increased and the waves were terrible, rising against each other, and so shaking and straining the vessel that she could make no headway and was in danger of being stove in. Seeing the great danger, the Admiral began to run before it. . . . The Admiral ordered that a pilgrimage should be made to Our Lady of Guadeloupe . . . and that all the crew should take an oath that the pilgrimage should be made by the man on whom the lot fell. As many beans as there were persons on board were obtained and on one a cross was cut with a knife. They were then put into a cap and shaken up. The first who put in his hand was the Admiral, and he drew out the bean with a cross so that the lot fell on him.

The *Pinta* and the *Nina* were separated during this storm and never met again until they reached harbour in Spain. By the time the storm was over they were all pledged to make a pilgrimage so that when they reached the Azores which belonged to Portugal the Admiral sent half the crew to fulfil their vow:

Sunday, 17th February Half of the crew then went in their shirts to carry out their vow. While they were at their prayers, all the people of the town, the cavalry and the foot soldiers with a captain at their head, came and took them all

prisoner. The Admiral, suspecting nothing, was waiting for the boat to take him and the rest to fulfil their vow. At 11 o'clock, seeing that they did not come back he weighed anchor, and made sail until he was in full view of the chapel. He saw many of the horsemen dismount and get into the boat with their weapons. They came out to the caravel to seize the Admiral so there was no other remedy but to go to sea. As there was a strong wind and a high sea, the Admiral says he was in much anxiety because he had only three sailors who knew their business. Soon afterwards the boat came alongside with five sailors, two priests and a scrivener who asked to be shown the commission granted them by the sovereigns of Castille. Then the Portuguese went on shore contented, and presently released all the crew and the boat.

They sailed on.

Sunday, 24th February . . . A squall hit the *Ǹina*, split all her sails, and put the rest of the vessel in great danger. Afterwards they ran under bare poles, owing to the force of the gale and the heavy sea.

Monday, 4th March During the night they were exposed to a terrible storm and expected to be overwhelmed by the cross-seas. The wind seemed to raise the caravel high in the air, and there was rain and lightning in several directions. When it was light, the Admiral recognised the land, which was the rock of Cintra, near the river of Lisbon, and decided to run in because there was nothing else he could do. Presently, the Admiral wrote to the King of Portugal stating that the sovereigns of Castille had ordered him to enter the ports of his Highness, to ask for what he required.

Columbus enjoyed a great triumph and he believed as did many people that he had reached the islands off China. He had read widely and had carefully calculated the size of the globe. His basic mistake was to believe that the distance from Europe to Asia was only 3,550 miles, when the real distance is 11,766 miles; therefore the West Indies were very close to where he expected to find Japan and China. Although he sailed to the West Indies on four more voyages and explored some of the coastline of South and Central America, he refused to admit that what he had discovered was a new world.

Adapted from
The Journal of the First Voyage of Columbus, translated and edited by Clements R. Markham (Hakluyt Society).
Select Documents Illustrating the Four Voyages of Columbus with an introduction by Cecil Jane and E. G. R. Taylor (Hakluyt Society).

Questions to consider

1. What frightened the sailors most on the voyage out?

2. What was Columbus' reason for marking down a smaller number of leagues than the real distance sailed in the course of a day?

3. Where did Columbus believe Cuba to be?

4. What pleased Columbus about the people he found on the West Indian Islands?

5. What things of value did Columbus find on the islands? Do you think the letter quoted on page 4 was accurate and fair?

6. What evidence did Columbus find suggesting that these islands were not the ones off the coasts of Japan and China?

7. Why do you think that Columbus continued to insist that he had reached Asia?

8. What was the most frightening part of the voyage home?

9. Try to imagine that you are one of the 39 men left behind on Hispaniola. What would you feel like when the Pinta and Nina sailed back to Europe?
What problems did you face? You will need to find out about the climate and vegetation of Hispaniola (now Haiti and the Dominican Republic).

11   The First Voyage Round the World

Ferdinand Magellan, a Portuguese navigator, wanted to search the coastline of South America for a strait joining the Atlantic and Pacific oceans, but could not persuade his king to finance him. He managed to interest Charles V of Spain in his scheme and entered his service. The Portuguese did not want the voyage to succeed because the Spanish would then be able to sail to the Spice Islands and end the Portuguese monopoly of this trade—the Portuguese would not allow people of other nations to use the African route they had discovered

A full account of the voyage was written by a member of the crew called Pigafetta and the extracts come from his journal.

Finally, after all the preparations had been made, the Captain-General (Magellan), a discreet and virtuous man still kept the destination of the voyage a secret so that the crew would not be filled with amazement and fear. The masters and captains of the other ships hated the Captain-General greatly, I don't know why unless it was because he was a Portuguese and they were Spaniards; these peoples have been rivals and borne each other ill will for a long time. In spite of this, they obeyed him.

On Monday, the 10th August in 1519, the fleet carrying 237 men in five ships [the *San Antonio* (120 tons), the *Trinidad* (110 tons), the *Conception* (90 tons), the *Victoria* (85 tons) and the *Santiago* (75 tons)] was ready to set sail from the mole of Seville. We came to the mouth of the river Guadalquivir carrying sail only on the foremast and firing all our artillery.

Artinano, *Arte de Navegar*, 1673. Museo Naval. Madrid

Magellan's flagship, the Victoria

What kind of ship is this?

At St. Lucar, the captain ordered all the men in the fleet to go to confession before we went any further, he set an example by leading the way. We set sail from St. Lucar and **on 26th of September** arrived at one of the Canary Islands where we remained three and a half days taking in provisions and other things we needed. After that we sailed to a port called Monterose where we stayed for two days supplying ourselves with pitch.

Sometimes we had contrary winds, sometimes we had good winds and at other times we had rain and no wind. We sailed for 60 days before we reached the equator, which was most unusual according to those who had navigated here several times. We crossed to a place called Verzin (Brazil) where we obtained fresh victuals including fowls, veal and various fruits.

Magellan followed the South American coast southwards and by Christmas was exploring the estuary of the River Plate in the hope of finding a strait. In March 1520, they headed south to Port Julian (49°S) where:

We entered a port to pass the winter and remained for two whole months without seeing anybody. However, one day, unexpectedly, we saw on the shore a giant who was quite naked and singing and dancing and leaping. He was so tall that the tallest of us only came up to his waist. His large face was painted red all over, his eyes were painted yellow and he had two hearts painted on his cheeks; he had but little hair and that was painted white. When he was brought before the captain, he was dressed in animal skins which were very skilfully sewn together. This giant wore shoes of animal skin on his feet and carried a short, thick bow in his hand; the bowstring was made of gut. He had a bundle of short, cane arrows which were feathered like ours although they were tipped with

black and white stones and not iron heads. The captain gave him food and drink, and then we showed him some things, a steel mirror amongst others. When the giant saw his reflection, he was greatly terrified, and leapt backwards knocking over three or four of our men.

We stayed in this port for about five months. As soon as we entered it, the masters of the other four ships plotted to put the Captain-General to death: they were Juan de Carthagena (who had been removed from captaincy of the *San Antonio* for refusing to carry out orders), the treasurer, Loys de Mendoza; Anthony Cocha, captain of the *Victoria*, and Gaspar de Casada of the *Conception*. However, the plot was discovered and the treasurer was stabbed to death with a dagger and quartered.

Casada was flayed alive while Carthagena was marooned and was never heard of again. They continued to search for a strait.

One of our ships, the *Santiago*, was lost exploring the coast but all the men were saved by a miracle; they were hardly wet. On the Day of Eleven Thousand Virgins (21st October), we found a strait that is 110 leagues long and less than half a league wide which opens into another sea, which is called the peaceful sea. It is surrounded by high, snow covered mountains.

Had it not been for the Captain-General, we would not have found the strait as the sailors thought there was no way of entering the peaceful sea. But the Captain-General said that he had seen a strait marked on a chart belonging to the King of Portugal and sent two ships, the *San Antonio* and the *Conception*, to look for its mouth while the other two ships, the flagship the *Trinidad* and the *Victoria*, waited for them in the Bay.

That night, we had a great storm which lasted until noon next day. We were forced to weigh anchor and let the ships go hither and thither about the Bay. The other two ships met such a headwind that they could not weather a cape near the end of the Bay. On approaching it, they saw a small opening, threw themselves into it, and so discovered the strait. Further on, they found a

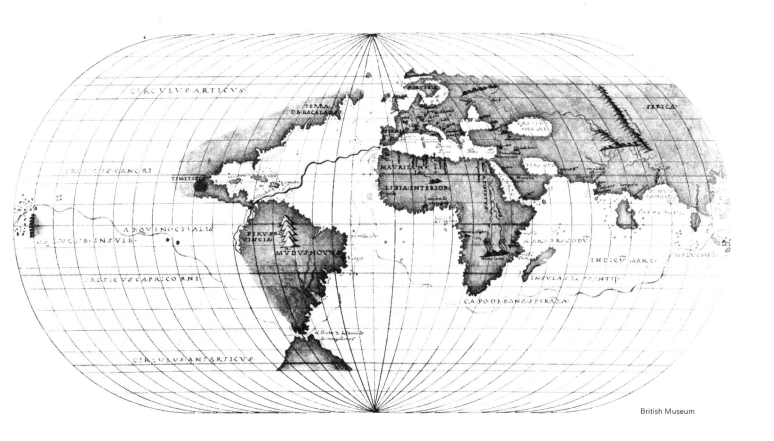

British Museum

A world map drawn by Battesta Agnese in Venice in 1536. It shows the route of the Victoria round the world.

The Straits of Magellan, from a book of about 1600. Which way is north?

bay and beyond that another strait and yet another bay which was much larger than the other two. Filled with joy, they returned to tell the Captain-General the good news. The Captain-General cried with joy and named this cape, the Cape of Desire. On entering the strait, we found two openings, one to the south-east and the other to the south-west. The Captain-General sent the *San Antonio* and the *Conception* to find out whether the south-east opening had an exit into the Pacific Sea. The *San Antonio* would not wait for the *Conception* because it intended to desert and return to Spain—which it did.

The *San Antonio* was Magellan's largest ship and carried most of the fleet's provisions. The loyal sailors wanted to turn back but Magellan insisted on them continuing.

On Wednesday, 28th November 1520, we came out of the strait into the Pacific Sea where we remained for three months and twenty days without being able to obtain fresh provisions. We ate old broken biscuit which was full of grubs and stinking from the dirt that the rats had made on it. We drank water that was yellow and stinking. We ate ox hides that were worn hard by the sun, the rain and the wind; we soaked them in the sea for four or five days and then cooked them on the embers of the fire. We ate sawdust and rats that cost half a ducado apiece and even then we could not get enough of them. Apart from these evils, the greatest misfortune was the swelling of the upper and lower gums of our men so that they could not eat. Many suffered from this disease and 19 died. Besides those that died, 25 to 30 others fell sick with the illness in their arms and legs, and in other places. Few men remained healthy; however, thanks be to the Lord, I had no sickness.

During those three months, we sailed in an open sea and ran fully four thousand leagues in the Pacific Sea. This was well named Pacific for during this time we met with no storm and saw no land except two small uninhabited islands in which we only found birds and trees. We called them the 'Unfortunate Islands'. If our Lord and his Mother had not aided us, we should all have died of hunger in this vast sea; I think no man will ever perform such a voyage again.

On Wednesday, 6th March, we discovered three islands, the 'Ladrones' or 'Thieves' (the Mariana Islands). The Captain-General wished to touch at the largest to get provisions, but it was impossible because the people climbed into the ships and robbed in such a way that one could not protect oneself from them. While we were striking and lowering the sails, they stole the skiff which was made fast to the poop of the Captain's ship. He was very angry and went ashore with 40 men, burnt 40 or 50 houses and some small boats and killed 7 men; we recovered our skiff.

They reached the Philippines. They were given a friendly welcome and spent Easter on the Island of Massava.

On Good Friday, the Captain sent our interpreter ashore to beg the King to sell us some provisions and to explain that we came to his country as friends not enemies. The King came out with 7 or 8 men in a boat and came aboard. He wore a cotton cloth worked with silk from his waist to his knees and carried a dagger with a long gold handle in a sheath of carved wood. He wore the perfumes of his country and his teeth were decorated with spots of gold so that his mouth seemed to be full of it.

He embraced the Captain and gave him three china dishes covered with leaves containing rice and two large fish called Dorades, and several other things. The Captain gave him a robe of red and yellow cloth, made in the Turkish fashion, and a very fine cap. To his people, he gave some knives and mirrors. After that refreshments were served. The Captain told the King through the interpreter that he wished to be friends. The King answered that he wanted the same thing. The Captain showed him cloths of various colours, linen, coral and much more merchandise. Then, he had some guns fired for him which astonished him greatly. The Captain stood one of his soldiers dressed in armour between three of his comrades who struck him with their swords and daggers, and told the King that a man dressed in white armour was worth 100 of his. The King said this was true and the Captain-General went on to say that each of his ships contained 200 similar soldiers.

The fleet sailed to Cebu where they successfully negotiated with the King and started trading.

The following Friday, we opened a shop full of merchandise which surprised them. For metal, iron, and other big goods, they paid us gold, and for small goods, they gave us rice, pigs, goats and other provisions.

Magellan visited the King.

The Captain, through an interpreter, tried to convert the King to the faith of Our Lord Jesus Christ. He told him that if he wished to be a good Christian, he must burn all his idols and replace them with crosses—that everyone should worship every day on their knees with their hands joined to heaven. He showed them how they ought to make the sign of the cross each day. The King and all his people answered that they would obey the commands of the Captain and do all that he told them. The Captain took the King by the hand and when he was baptised, named him Don Charles after the Emperor, his sovereign. He then asked the King to swear that he would always be obedient and faithful to the King of Spain, and he took the oath.

In eight days, all the inhabitants of this island were baptised and some belonging to neighbouring islands.

On Friday, 26th April, Zula, one of the principal men or chiefs of the island of Matan, sent word to the Captain to say that if he did not do all that he had promised, it was because another chief called Silapulapu prevented him from doing so: but that if on the following night the Captain would send him one boatful of men, he would fight and subdue his rival. The Captain decided to go himself with three boats. We entreated him not to go on this enterprise but he was a good shepherd and would not abandon his flock.

We left Cebu at midnight, we were 60 men armed with breastplates and helmets. We reached Mathan three hours before daylight and waited until dawn before leaping into water up to our thighs and wading across two long bowshots of water to the shore. We found the islanders, 1,000 in number, drawn up in three squadrons: two squadrons attacked our flanks and the third our front. They charged down on us with terrible shouts. Our musketeers and crossbowmen fired for half an hour from a distance but achieved nothing as

their bullets and arrows passed through the wooden shields and may have wounded their arms but did not stop them—they charged us with greater fury. Seeing that our bodies were well

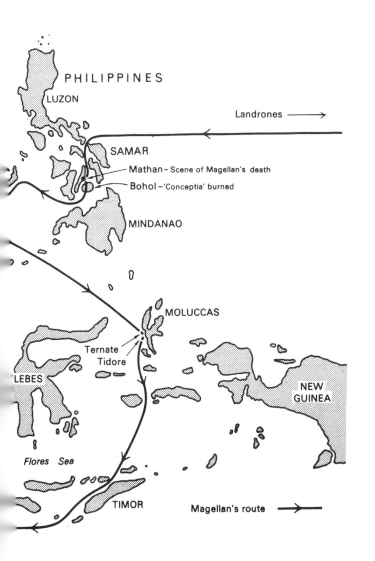

PHILIPPINES

LUZON

Landrones ⟶

SAMAR

Mathan – Scene of Magellan's death

Bohol – 'Conceptia' burned

MINDANAO

MOLUCCAS

Ternate
Tidore

LEBES

NEW
GUINEA

Flores Sea

TIMOR

Magellan's route ⟶

INSVLA MATHAN

Victoria

Levinus Hulsius. *Voyages.* c.1600. Bodleian Library

Sketch map of the East Indies, showing the route of
the *Victoria*. The picture shows the battle in which
Magellan was killed.

defended but our legs were bare, they aimed at
them. The Captain had his right leg pierced by a
poisoned arrow and had to order us to retreat by
degrees; but most of our men fled leaving only 6
to 8 of us with him. He, like a good knight,
remained at his post without retreating further.
Thus we fought for more than an hour until an
Indian succeeded in thrusting a cane lance into

the Captain's face. All our enemies rushed at him and one of them, armed with a large sword like a scimitar, struck him a great blow on the left leg which brought him down on his face. Then, the Indians threw themselves upon him with lances and swords so that they deprived of life our mirror, light, comfort and true guide. This fatal battle was fought **on 27th April, 1521.**

We then elected in the place of the Captain, Duarte Barbosa, a Portuguese and a relation of the Captain's, and Juan Serrano, a Spaniard.

The King of Cebu turned on the sailors and Serrano and a party of 24 men were cut off. The Spanish burnt the *Conception* as there were not enough men to work three ships.

We then took a S.S.W. course and arrived at a large island (Mindanao in the Philippines). Continuing our voyage, we changed course between west and north-west and after running 25 leagues, reached a large island called Palawan. Here, we found pigs, goats, fowls, yams and bananas of various kinds: some are half a cubit long and as thick as one's arm, others are only a span long and others are still smaller—these are the best. They have cocoa nuts, sugar canes and roots like turnips. In short, we found this island to be a paradise.

Sailing from Palawan to the S.W., we reached Borneo after a run of ten leagues. The King to whom we presented ourselves is a Moslem and is called Raja Siripada; he is about 40 years old and rather fat. This city (Bruni) is entirely built on foundations laid in salt water, except for the houses of the King and some of the great princes; it contains 25,000 fires or families. The houses are made of wood and placed on great piles to raise them up high. At high tide, the women row through the city selling provisions and necessities. Around the King's house, there is a wall made of great bricks with bastions containing 56 bronze bombards and 6 iron ones.

On Monday, 29th July, we saw more than 100 ships coming towards us. Fearing treachery, we hurriedly set sail.

On Wednesday, 6th November, we discovered four rather high islands 14 leagues to the east. The native pilot told us that these were the Moluccas for which we gave thanks to God and fired all our cannon to comfort ourselves. It need not cause wonder that we were so happy as we had spent 27 months less 2 days searching for them.

Friday, 8th November, three hours before sunset, we entered a port on the island of Tidore. Next day, the King of the island approached the ships in his boat so we showed him respect by meeting him. He was sitting under a silk umbrella with his son in front of him holding the royal sceptre. There were two men with gold pitchers of water so that he could wash his hands and two more with gold boxes of betel nut—his teeth were very red from chewing it. This King has a handsome appearance. He wore a shirt of fine white cloth, the sleeves embroidered with gold, and a wrapper which reached from his waist to the ground. His feet were bare. Round his head he wore a veil and a garland of flowers. His name is Rajah Manzor. He promised to give us cloves and become a subject of King Charles.

On Tuesday, 12th November, the King had a house built in the city for our merchandise. We carried all that we had to barter there and trading began at once.

A later picture of Europeans trading with people on one of the islands in the East Indies. What are the Europeans trying to sell? What do you think the East Indians are offering in exchange?

De Bry. *Voyages*. c.1600. Bodleian Library

On Wednesday, 27th November, the king issued a proclamation that whoever had cloves might sell them to us. All that and the following day, we bought cloves like mad.

During their stay in Tidore, they heard that the Portuguese had sent out a fleet to arrest them (see p. 1). They filled their holds, bent on their new sails and prepared to leave for home.

By Wednesday morning, everything was ready for our departure from the Moluccas. The *Victoria* made sail and stood out a little, waiting for the *Trinidad* which had difficulty getting up her anchor. The sailors noticed that she was leaking badly in the hold so the *Victoria* returned to her anchorage. They began to unload the *Trinidad*'s cargo to see if the leak could be stopped. The water poured in with great force and we were unable to find the leak. All that day and the next, we did nothing else but work at the pumps but without success. We on the *Victoria* feared that her seams might open because of the weight of the cargo and the length of the voyage; we lightened her by unloading 60 hundredweights of cloves which were carried to the house where the crew of the *Trinidad* lodged. Some of our men preferred to stay in the Moluccas because they thought that the ship could not endure so long a voyage and remembering how much they had suffered on the outward journey, they feared to die of hunger in mid-ocean.

Fifty-four men remained in Tidore as a garrison to prepare for future Spanish expeditions. The rest of the men divided into two crews. One set off in the *Trinidad* back across the Pacific but was captured by the Portuguese. The other, led by Sebastian del Cano, sailed across the Indian Ocean in the *Victoria* and approached the southern tip of Africa.

In order to round the Cape of Good Hope, we went as far as latitude 42° south. We stayed off that cape for 9 weeks with sails struck while Westerly and North-Westerly gales beat against our bows. Some of our men, among them the sick, would have liked to land at a place called Mozambique belonging to the Portuguese, because the ship made so much water and because of the great cold we suffered, but mostly because we had nothing but rice and water to eat and drink, all our meat having rotted through lack of salt. But the greater number of us, prizing honour more than life itself, decided on attempting at any risk to return to Spain.

At length, with the aid of God, we passed that terrible cape but were forced to come within 5 leagues of it or else we should never have rounded it. We sailed North-East for two whole months without rest. In this short time, we lost 21 men.

Compelled by extreme necessity, we decided to call at the Cape Verde Islands. **On Wednesday, 9th July,** we reached one of the islands called St. James. Knowing that we were in an enemy's country, on sending the seamen ashore to get victuals, we told them to inform the Portuguese that we had sprung our foremast at the Equator and that our ship was alone, as whilst we tried to repair it, the Captain-General had gone on with the other two ships to Spain. In exchange for some of our merchandise, we obtained two boatloads of rice. On returning for some more, the boat was detained with 13 men in it. Seeing that and from the movement in some caravels, suspecting that they wished to capture us, we set sail at once.

At last, when it pleased Heaven, **on Saturday, 6th September,** of the year 1522, we entered the

Bay of St. Lucar; of the 60 men that made up our crew when we left Tidore but 18 remained and these for the most part were sick. From the day we left this bay of St. Lucar until our return thither, we reckoned that we had run more than 14,460 leagues, and had sailed round the earth from east to west.

At this moment of triumph, Pigafetta did not forget Magellan.

He died but I trust that your illustrious Highness will not allow his memory to be forgotten, so much the more since I see also in you the virtues of our great Captain, for one of his was constancy in ill fortune. In the midst of the sea he was able to endure hunger better than we. Most versed in nautical charts, he knew better than others the true art of navigation. It is certain proof of this that by his own genius and courage without any-one giving him an example, he so nearly completed the circuit of the globe.

Adapted from *The First Voyage Round the World by Magellan* translated from the accounts of Pigafetta by Lord Stanley of Alderley (Hakluyt Society).

Ferdinand Magellan—an engraving.

Questions to consider

Why did Magellan not tell the crew where they were going? What did the captains of the other ships think of him?

How was the strait to the Pacific discovered?

Why do you think that the 'San Antonio' deserted the rest of the fleet?

How did the sailors eke out their scanty stores during their passage of the Pacific?
What does Pigafetta tell us of the rulers of the Spice Islands?

Why did some of the crew stay in Tidore? Imagine that you are a member of del Cano's crew and explain why you decided either to remain on the island or to sail home with him.

Write an obituary for Magellan.

12 The Conquest of Mexico by Cortes

After Columbus' first voyage to the West Indies, various sailors explored the coasts of mainland America, and rumours circulated about 'strange looking towers or pyramids, ascended by stone steps' and 'the people who came out in canoes to watch the ships clad in quilted cotton doublets and wearing cloaks and brilliant plumes'. The Spaniards settled in the West Indies and the Governor of Cuba, Don Diego Velasquez, was determined to conquer the mainland. He placed Hernando Cortes in charge of the arrangements for an expedition. Born in 1485, Cortes was the son of a poor country gentleman; he had studied at Salamanca University, and crossed over to the West Indies in 1504. He was fiercely ambitious and so the suspicious Velasquez tried unsuccessfully to replace him. A small armada sailed on 10th February 1519 carrying 508 soldiers, 100 sailors, 16 horses, 32 crossbows, 13 arquebuses (hand guns), and several small cannon. The following account of Cortes' adventures is taken from his 'Five Letters to Charles V'.

At the beginning of the expedition, Cortes made an address to his men to fire their imaginations:

> I hold out to you a glorious prize, but it is to be won by incessant toil. Great things are achieved only by great exertions, and glory was never the reward of sloth. If I have laboured hard and staked my all on this undertaking, it is for the love of that renown, which is the noblest recompense of man. But if any among you covet riches more, be true to me, as I will make you masters of such as our countrymen have never dreamed of. You are few in number, but strong in resolution; doubt not but that the Almighty, who has never deserted the Spaniard in his contest with the infidel (the unbelievers), will shield you, for your cause is a just cause, and you are to fight under the banner of the Cross.

After some early landings, Cortes finally chose a base.

> Having built a wooden town, I (Cortes) left the city with 15 horsemen and 300 foot soldiers, all equipped for war as best as I was able and time permitted. I left in the town of Vera Cruz, 2

Cortes, an engraving from a contemporary portrait

Prescott, *Conquest of Mexico*. 1890

horsemen and 150 foot soldiers, engaged in building a fort. There were those who wanted to leave on seeing how large and populous the country was, while we Spaniards were so few. Believing that if I left the ships there, they would revolt with them and I would be left almost alone, I determined, on the pretext that they were unseaworthy, to have the ships beached and burnt. Thus everybody lost hope of ever leaving the country, and I set out on my march without fear that when I turned my back, the people left in the town would fail me.

At first, the Indians treated the Spaniards with suspicion and fear, but their armour, canon, and horses (there were no horses in America) seemed to mark them out as the long expected companions of the legendary god, Quetzalcoatli. Many centuries earlier, this god had come to Mexico with his white faced bearded followers and had ruled it wisely and well; then the Mexican Indians had turned against them and driven them out; Quetzalcoatli had sworn to return and punish them.

The Indians, including the Aztecs, were unable to make up their minds about the Spaniards: if they were strangers from a land across the sea they could be attacked and destroyed, but if they were the returning gods, they must be respected and obeyed. The Indian tribes were dominated by the warrior Aztecs who forced them to pay tribute in gold, food, and people—the people were sacrificed to the gods. So many of the tribes joined Cortes and provided him with supplies, bearers and soldiers.

Cortes described the Indians:

The people who inhabit this country are a people of middle size with well proportioned bodies and features, except that in each province their customs differ: some pierce their ears and put large and ugly objects in them, others pierce their nostrils down to the mouth, and still others pierce their lips as far as their gums and hang from them large round stones or pieces of gold, so weighty that they pull down the lower lip and make it appear deformed. The clothing they wear is like long veils, very curiously worked. The men wear breech cloths about their bodies and very thin large cloaks painted in the Moorish style. The women of the ordinary people wear painted clothes reaching from their waists to their feet. There are also houses like barbers' shops where they wash their heads and shave themselves; there are also baths. Finally good order and politeness prevail for they are a people full of understanding and intelligence. There are many lords living in the towns and the people who are tillers of the soil are their vassals; though each one has his own lands, some have more than others. When undertaking wars, they all gather together, and thus assembled decide and plan them.

Montezuma, the Aztec ruler of Mexico, heard reports of the successes of the Spaniards. He could not make up his mind whether they were ordinary invaders or the gods from the East that the ancient legends spoke of. Cortes reported to Charles V that:

There came to me 6 lords from amongst the principal vassals of Montezuma accompanied by about 200 retainers to tell me that they came on the part of Montezuma to say that he wished to be a vassal of Your Highness and my friend. He sent word that I should say what I wanted him to give your Highness as an annual tribute of gold, silver, precious stones, slaves, cotton and wearing apparel, and other possessions; and that he would give it all if only I would not come to his country.

Cortes meeting Montezuma's messengers

Spaniards marching towards Tenochtitlan

Montezuma and the City of Tenochtitlan

The Spaniards made their way through the mountains to the great volcanic valley of Mexico:

This province is circular and completely surrounded by high and rugged mountains. Its plain is perhaps 70 leagues in circumference and there are two lakes: one is of fresh water and the other larger one is salt. The lakes are divided from one another by a small chain of very high hills. Communication between one lake and the other, and between the city and the other towns round about, is by means of canoes with no need of going by land.

After the Spaniards had surveyed the view of the valley and city, they marched down to meet Montezuma.

We were received by the lord Montezuma accompanied by 200 chiefs, barefoot and very richly dressed in a kind of uniform. According to their custom, Montezuma walked in the middle of the

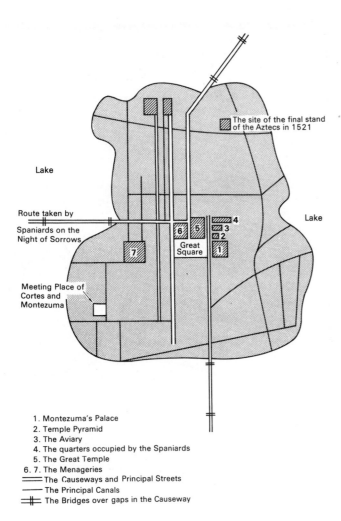

The site of the final stand
of the Aztecs in 1521

Lake

Route taken by
Spaniards on the
Night of Sorrows

Lake

4
3
6 **5** **2**
Great
Square **1**

7

Meeting Place of
Cortes and
Montezuma

1. Montezuma's Palace
2. Temple Pyramid
3. The Aviary
4. The quarters occupied by the Spaniards
5. The Great Temple
6. 7. The Menageries
═══ The Causeways and Principal Streets
─── The Principal Canals
╪╪╪ The Bridges over gaps in the Causeway

Plan of Tenochtitlan

street with two lords, one on the right side and one on the left, each supporting him with their arms beneath a marvellously rich canopy of green feathers with much gold and silver embroidery, which was wonderful to look at. As we approached each other, I descended from my horse and was about to embrace him but the two lords in attendance prevented me. I took off a collar of pearls and diamonds that I wore and put it round his neck. After we had gone through some of the streets, one of his servants came to me with two collars made of coloured shells.

After this happy meeting, Cortes was given excellent quarters and thought out his position very carefully.

I determined to seize him (Montezuma) and confine him in my quarters so I stationed sufficient guards in the streets and went to the palace of Montezuma to see him as I had done on previous occasions. After conversing lightly on pleasant subjects, I told Montezuma that I was very grateful for all that he had done for us and that all that now remained was for him to live in my quarters. Finally, he agreed to come with me to prevent bloodshed. Thus we went to my quarters without causing any commotion in the city.

The great city of Tenochtitlan (Mexico City) is built on the salt lake, and from the mainland to the city is a distance of 2 leagues. It has three approaches by means of artificial causeways which are two cavalry lances in width. The city is as large as Seville or Cordoba. Its streets (I speak of the principal ones) are very broad and straight; some of these and all of the other roads are bordered by canals on which they go about in canoes. All the streets have gaps at regular intervals to let the water flow from one canal to another, and at all these openings, (some of which are very broad), there are bridges which are very large, strong and well constructed, over which as many as 10 horsemen can ride abreast. Perceiving that if the inhabitants wished to practise any treachery against us, they might by raising the bridges at the exits and entrances starve us without our being able to reach land, I made great haste to build 4 brigantines (small sailing ships) capable of taking 300 men and horses to land.

The city has many squares where markets are held and trading is carried on. There is one square, twice as large as that of Salamanca, all surrounded by arcades, where daily more than 60,000 souls buy and sell, and where all the kinds of merchandise produced in these countries are found including food products, jewels of gold and silver, lead, brass, copper, stone, bones, shells and feathers. A large amount of good quality chinaware is sold including earthen jars of every size for holding liquids, pitchers, pots, tiles—all made of very special clay and almost all decorated and painted in some way. Maize is sold both as grain and in the form of bread and is vastly superior both in the size of the ear and in taste to that of all the islands and the rest of the mainland. Pasties made from game and fish pies may be seen on sale. Eggs from hens, geese and other birds may be had and likewise omelettes ready made. A very fine building in the great square serves as a kind of court where 10 or 12 judges are always seated to hear cases arising in the market and pass sentence on evildoers.

This great city contains many temples or houses for idols, very beautiful buildings, situated in different districts. Priests live in the most important of these, so that in addition to the actual temples

Aztec temple

Florentine Codex. Laurentian Library, Florence

there are comfortable lodgings. All the priests dress in black and never cut their hair from the time they enter their religious order until they leave it. Amongst these temples, there is one which no human tongue is able to describe, because it is so large that within its walls a village of 500 houses could easily be built. Inside it, there are some excellent buildings where the priests live. There are some 40 tall and well built towers. All these towers are places of burial for the chiefs and each one is dedicated to the idol to which they were particularly devoted. The greatest of these idols in which they have the most faith I overturned from their seats and rolled down the stairs; I had the chapels where they were kept scrubbed out as they were full of blood from the human sacrifices. I set up images of Our Lady and other Saints in them which upset Montezuma and the natives not a little. I instructed them

Florentine Codex. Laurentian Library, Florence

Cortes speaking through an interpreter

through my interpreters that there was but one God, Lord of all, who had created the sky, the earth and all things. I forbade them to sacrifice human beings to their idols and during the whole time I was in the city not a single soul was known to be killed.

The city contains many large and fine houses as all the nobles owing allegiance to Montezuma have their houses in the city and live there part of the year, and in addition there are many rich citizens who have fine houses. All have very delightful flower gardens of every kind, both on the ground floors and on the upper storeys. Along the causeways which lead to the city, there are two stone pipes, each two paces broad and five feet deep; through one of which flows very good fresh water to the heart of the city, which all can use and drink. The other pipe is empty and is used

when the first one is being cleaned. Montezuma had a palace where there was a beautiful garden with balconies overhanging it, the pillars and flagstones of which were of jasper beautifully worked. In this palace there was room to lodge two great princes and all their servants. It had ten pools of water in which every kind of waterfowl was kept.

Montezuma continued to receive his chiefs while he remained a prisoner in Cortes' palace, and all went well until bad news reached Cortes from the coast. Cortes wrote:

I learned that the armada and people who arrived in Vera Cruz belonged to Diego Velasquez (Governor of Cuba) and had come by his order under a certain Panfilo de Narvaez as their captain. As I saw that discontent was spreading, and the country was rising on account of Narvaez, it appeared to me that by going to him myself all might be settled. I therefore started the same day, leaving the garrison well provided with maize and water; the garrison consisted of some 500 men (including the Indian allies) and some cannon.

Cortes met up with Narvaez, who had been sent to arrest him, and defeated him; the Governor's army joined him when they heard of the treasures that could be theirs. However, while he was engaged in dealing with this threat to his authority, his second-in-command in Tenochtitlan, Alvarada, invited a number of Aztec chiefs to a feast on one of their holy days and massacred them. The Indians rose and surrounded the fort; Cortes wrote:

The Indians had attacked the fort on all sides and set fire to it in many places. In the fight, the Indians captured a great part of the provisions I had left them, and had burned my four brigantines. My men were in extreme need and begged me for the love of God to come to their succour in all possible haste.

Cortes marched back to Tenochtitlan and joined the garrison. He continued:

Montezuma, who with one of his sons and many other chiefs, was still a prisoner, asked to be carried to the roof of the fort where he could speak to the Indian captains and people and call for an end to the fighting. I had him taken thither, but when he reached the parapet on the top of the fort, one of his own subjects struck him on the head with a stone with such force that he died after three days. I then had him taken out, dead as he was, by two of the Indian prisoners, who carried him away to his people.

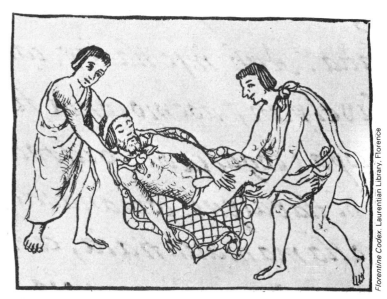

Florentine Codex. Laurentian Library, Florence

Death of Montezuma

The death of Montezuma made reconciliation impossible and Cortes prepared to fight his way out of Tenochtitlan; this is known as 'the Night of Sorrow'.

Having abandoned our fort and much treasure belonging not only to Your Majesty but also to the Spaniards and myself, I set forth as secretly as possible taking with me a son and two daughters of Montezuma. When we reached the gaps in the causeway (the Indians had taken the bridges away), we laid down the wooden bridge we had made and crossed over with little difficulty as there were none to offer resistance except a few watchmen who shouted so loudly that by the time we came to the second gap, there was an infinite multitude of the enemy battling on every side, both on land and water. I crossed rapidly with 5 horsemen and 500 foot soldiers and we proceeded

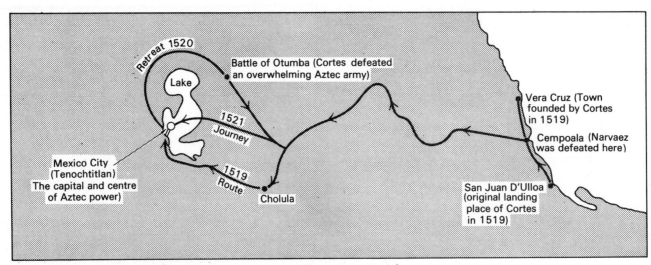

Part of Mexico showing Cortes' journeys to and from Tenochtitlan.

to swim across all the other gaps until we reached the mainland. Leaving these men here, I returned to the others and found that they were fighting stoutly, but the casualties our men sustained were beyond calculation, not only the Spaniards but our Indian Allies who were with us. Though the Spaniards killed many natives, many of them were killed, many horses were lost, and all the gold and jewels and many other things which we carried and all the artillery was lost.

Cortes Second Expedition

Once on the mainland, the Spaniards fought their way through the mountains defeating a much larger Aztec Army at Otumba, and finally reached Vera Cruz. Another expedition was prepared and Cortes led a much larger and better equipped army—some 500 horsemen and 1,000 foot soldiers—back to Tenochtitlan—the Aztecs made little attempt to stop them but waited in the city. Cortes had a fleet of brigantines built so that the city was cut off from the mainland. Then, a cruel struggle took place as the Indians defended every inch of their city against the invader. Cortes describes one of many battles between the Indians and Spaniards.

After having heard Mass and having instructed the captains, I left our quarters with 15 or 20 horsemen, 300 Spanish foot soldiers and all our Indian Allies, and advanced along the causeway. We found the enemy already waiting for us, yelling fiercely. During the preceding three days there had been no fighting so they had been able to open up the gaps in the causeway and make them more

Spanish horseman

Florentine Codex. Laurentian Library, Florence

Spanish foot soldier

Florentine Codex. Laurentian Library, Florence

Florentine Codex. Laurentian Library, Florence

Spaniards, led by Indian ally, crossing the causeway compare the weapons of the Spaniards with those of the Aztecs

Spaniards attacking Tenochtitlan

dangerous to attack. The brigantines accompanied us on both sides of the causeway as they could sail very close to the enemy and do great damage with their cannon, muskets and crossbows. Discovering this, our men landed and captured the breastworks they had thrown up. We pursued the enemy who immediately fortified themselves behind the other breastworks they had prepared, which we captured although with greater difficulty and danger than before. We drove them from the streets and square where the great houses of the city stand. Then, I ordered that no Spaniard should leave while I and our Allies filled up all the gaps in the causeway with stone and bricks. This was such a labour that although we had 10,000 Indians helping us, it was already the hour of Vespers (6 o'clock) before we had finished making the repairs. During all this time, the Spaniards and our Allies were constantly fighting the enemy.

The Aztecs fought with ever increasing determination and occasionally won a victory.

The moment I reached that wretched bridge, I saw the Spaniards fleeing towards us with the enemy setting on them like dogs. Seeing that disaster threatened, I began to cry 'Stop, stop', but when I arrived at the water, I found it so full of Spaniards and Indians that I could not have put a straw into it. We all gathered in the square but the enemy charged us so furiously that it was all we could to do to keep them off. Immediately afterwards, in one of the pyramids of their idols, they offered up many perfumes and incenses as a sign of victory. In this victory, the enemy killed 35 or 40 Spaniards and more than a 1,000 Indians as well as wounding another 20 Christians—I was wounded myself in one leg. After the victory, the defenders took all the living and dead Spaniards they had captured to their main temple, and in some lofty towers there, they stripped them and sacrificed them, opening their breasts and taking out their hearts to offer them to their idols.

Seeing the way things were going and that already more than 45 days had been spent in this siege, I determined to take measures for our security and for the weakening of the foe. These consisted of our gaining the streets of the city and demolishing all the houses on both sides, henceforward we would not go one step forward without levelling everything, so that which was water was made dry land however much time it took.

On 13th August 1521, the Aztecs were forced to surrender.

It pleased God that the captain of a brigantine called Garci Holguin overtook a canoe in which there were some distinguished people. They signalled to him not to shoot because their king was there. Quatamucin (the last of the Aztec kings) stood up in the canoe saying 'I am the king of Tenochtitlan and of this country, take me to Cortes. I ask only that my wife and children be spared.'

The warrior race of the Aztecs was virtually destroyed although their traditions lived on and reappeared in bloody risings against the Spaniards. Their buildings were mostly demolished and their masterpieces of gold and silver work disappeared into the melting pot to finance Spanish wars in Europe. The old religion was banned and Christian missionaries set to work to convert the Indians.

Adapted from Francis MacNutt, *The Five Letters of Cortes to Charles V* (Putnam).

The pictures in this pamphlet were drawn by Aztecs shortly after their defeat by the Spaniards, and were published as illustrations in a Spanish history.

Suggestions for practical work

1. Make drawings/paintings or a frieze of the Indian men and women.
2. Make a plan, drawing, or model of Tenochtitlan.

Questions to consider

Write a 'guide' to the old city of Tenochtitlan under headings such as—buildings, bridges, water supply, gardens, markets, food . . . . . .

Put yourself in the place of an Aztec Indian and describe the Spanish soldiers. Then tell of some of the things that Cortes and his soldiers did in Mexico.

Why did Montezuma find it so difficult to decide what to do about the Spaniards? How did he treat them at first?

Why did Cortes kidnap Montezuma and why did Montezuma allow him to do so?

What happened to Montezuma in the end? What kind of person do you think he was?

Imagine that you are an Aztec child in Tenochtitlan. Describe what you saw of the last fight for the city.

13 The Second Voyage of Jacques Cartier in 1536

The discovery of America inspired many Europeans to sail westwards; the French played a particularly important part in the exploration of North America. French fishermen had been visiting the rich fishing grounds of the Grand Banks off Newfoundland since the beginning of the sixteenth century. In 1534, Jacques Cartier sailed from St Malo to search for a route to Cathay round North America, and to discover certain islands and lands where it was said that a great quantity of gold and other precious things were to be found. He reached Newfoundland and sailed along its northern coast, passed through the strait of Belle Isle into the Gulf of the St. Lawrence, and landed on the Gaspé peninsula where he met the chief of the Saguenay Indians, Donnacona. When he returned to France, the chief's sons, Taignoagnuy and Dom Agaya, agreed to accompany him. Encouraged by their descriptions of Canada, King Francis I financed a second voyage in 1535.

The following extracts are taken from the account of Cartier's second voyage, 1535/6 :

On Sunday, 16th May, the day and feast of Whitsuntide, in the year 1535 by command of the Captain and the willing consent of all, each confessed himself and we all took communion together in the cathedral of St. Malo. Afterwards we went and knelt in the choir of the church before the Bishop who gave us his blessing.

On the following Wednesday, **19th May,** the wind came fair and in our favour and we set sail with three vessels, namely *Grande Hermine* of some 100 to 120 tons burden, on board of which sailed the Commander with Thomas Fromont as mate. In the second ship, called *Petit Hermine* of about 60 tons' burden Mace Jalobert went as captain under Cartier, with William le Marie as mate; and as captain of the third and smallest vessel, named *Emérillon* of some 40 tons burden, went William le Breton with Jacques Mainguard as mate. We sailed in fine weather until **Wednesday, 26th May,** when it turned bad and stormy and continued so for such a long time with incessant headwinds and overcast sky that no ships that have crossed the ocean ever had more of it; so much that on **Friday, 25th June,** on account of this bad weather and lowering sky, we all three became separated and had no news of one another until we reached Newfoundland, where we had agreed to meet.

Here we refitted and took on board wood, fresh water and other necessaries. At daybreak on **Thursday, the 29th** of that month, we made sail and got under way to continue our voyage; and headed along the north shore of the Gulf which ran E.N.E. and W.S.W., until about 8 o'clock in the evening when we lowered sail opposite two islands.

They cruised along the coast from island to island until they discovered the mouth of the River of Hochelega (the St. Lawrence) and then turned back for a time 'to make sure that no strait existed along the North Shore.' They discovered :

. . . a fresh water river (the Moisie) which enters the Gulf with such force that at a distance of more than a league from the shore, the water is as fresh as spring water. We entered this river with our longboats and at the mouth of it found a depth of only a fathom and a half. Up this river were several fish in appearance like horses (Walruses)

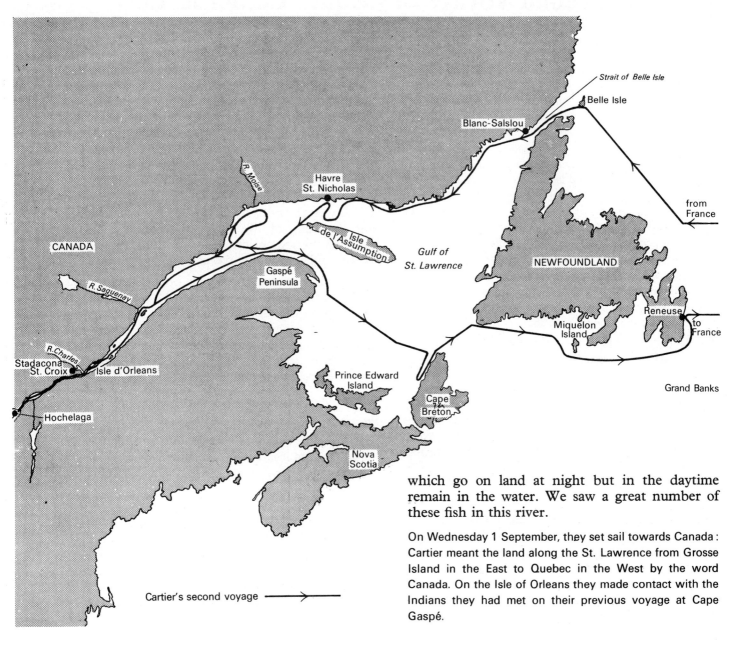

Strait of Belle Isle

Belle Isle

Blanc-Salslou

from France

R. Moise

Havre St. Nicholas

Isle de l'Assumption

CANADA

Gulf of St. Lawrence

NEWFOUNDLAND

R. Saguenay

Gaspé Peninsula

Reneuse

to France

R. Charles
Stadacona
St. Croix

Isle d'Orleans

Miquelon Island

Prince Edward Island

Grand Banks

Hochelaga

Cape Breton

Nova Scotia

Cartier's second voyage ———→

which go on land at night but in the daytime remain in the water. We saw a great number of these fish in this river.

On Wednesday 1 September, they set sail towards Canada: Cartier meant the land along the St. Lawrence from Grosse Island in the East to Quebec in the West by the word Canada. On the Isle of Orleans they made contact with the Indians they had met on their previous voyage at Cape Gaspé.

We went on land and took with us the two Indians we had seized on our former voyage. We came upon several of the people of the country who began to run away and would not come near until our two Indians had spoken to them; when they knew who they were, they began to welcome them, dancing and going through many ceremonies. Some of the headmen came to our longboats bringing us many eels and other fish with two or three measures of Indian corn and many large melons. During that day, many canoes filled with the people of the country, both men and women, came to our ships to see and welcome our two Indians. The Commander received them well and treated them to what he had to offer. To ingratiate himself with them, he gave them some small presents of little value at which they were much pleased.

On the morrow (Wednesday, 8th September), the lord of Canada, named Donnacona, came to our ships accompanied by many Indians in twelve canoes. When he was opposite to the smallest of our three ships, this chief began to speak to us moving his body and limbs in a marvellous manner, as is their custom when showing joy and contentment. When he came abreast of the Commander's vessels, on board of which were the two Indians who were his sons—Taignoagny and Dom Agaya—the chief spoke to them and they to him, telling him what they had seen in France and about the good treatment meted out to them there. At this the chief was much pleased and begged the Commander to stretch out his arms that he might hug and kiss them, which is the way they welcome one in that country. After this the Commander stepped down into this chief's canoe, and ordered bread and wine to be brought so that the chief and his Indians might eat some. When

this had been done they were much pleased but no other present was then given to the chief pending a more suitable time and place. After these things had been carried out, they took leave of each other and separated.

After a few days, they sailed as far as the St. Croix (St. Charles) river, where they found the village of Stadacona. The Indians tried to stop them penetrating further up the river. Cartier was determined to continue and so the Indians staged a dramatic scene.

On the next day, the 18th of the month, they staged a great scene to prevent us from going to Hochelaga (the capital of a neighbouring tribe). They dressed up three Indians as devils, arraying them in black and white dogskins, with horns as long as one's arm and their faces coloured black as coal, and unknown to us put them in a canoe. At that hour the Indians all came out of the wood and showed themselves in front of our ships but without coming as near as they were in the habit of doing. Soon after the canoe arrived with the three Indians dressed as devils. As they drew near, the one in the middle made a wonderful speech; when he finished the chief Donnacona and his people at once seized the canoe and carried them into the wood. The Commander, seeing their grimaces and gestures, asked them what was the matter. They replied that there was bad news, that their god, Cadouagny by name, had made an announcement at Hochelaga, and that the three Indians had come in his name to tell them that there would be so much ice and snow that we would all perish. At this we began to laugh and to tell them that their god Cudouagny was a mere fool who did not know what he was saying; and that Jesus would keep them safe if they would trust in Him.

The following day, **Sunday, 19th September**, we made sail and got under way with the bark (*Emérillon*) and the two longboats to push up river with the tide. Along both shores we had sight of the finest and most beautiful land it is possible to see, being as level as a pond and covered with the most magnificent trees in the world. On the banks were so many vines loaded with grapes that it seems that they could only have been planted by husbandmen, but because they are never looked after or pruned, the grapes are not so sweet nor so large as our own. We also noticed a large number of huts along the banks of the river, which are inhabited by Indians who catch great quantities of the numerous fish in the river according to the season.

Some miles further up river, they had to leave the bark and continue in the longboats until, on 2 October, they reached Hochelaga, which was an Indian village on the island of Montreal. Here they received a very friendly welcome. They seem to have been regarded as gods as the women brought their children to touch them and there was dancing throughout the night in the light of great wood fires. The next morning, Cartier 'dressed himself splendidly' and accompanied by a well armed group of his men marched through well cultivated fields of Indian corn to the most impressive Indian village they had yet seen.

The Village is circular and is completely enclosed by a wooden palisade which is well joined and lashed after their manner and is some two lances high (about 20 feet). There is only one gate and entrance to this village and that can be barred up. Over this gate and in many places about the enclosure, there are galleries (covered parapet walks) with ladders for mounting them; these galleries are provided with rocks and stones for the defence and protection of the place. There are

some 50 houses in this village, each about 50 or more paces in length and 12 or 15 in width, built completely of wood and covered in and boarded up with large pieces of the bark and rind of trees which are well and cunningly lashed together in their own manner. Inside these houses are many rooms and chambers, and in the middle is a large

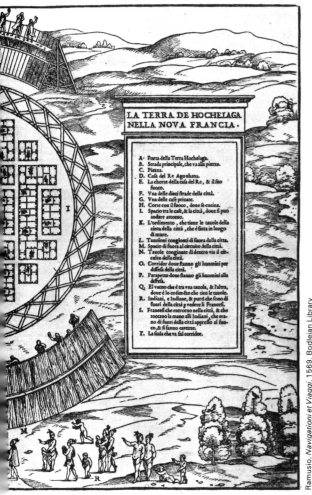

This plan of Hochelaga comes from an Italian book of voyages, 1569.

store the corn of which they make their bread.

They have wooden mortars like those used in France and in these they pound the corn into flour with wooden pestles. This they knead into dough of which they make small loaves, which are set on a broad hot stone and then covered with hot pebbles. This is the way they bake their bread having no ovens. They also make many kinds of soup with this corn, with beans and peas of which they have a considerable supply, and with large cucumbers and other fruits. They have in their houses also large vessels like cauldrons in which they place their fish, such as eels and others, that are smoked during the summer, and on these they live during the winter. They make a great store of these as we ourselves saw.

While the Europeans were looking about them the Indians carried their chief towards them on a litter. He alighted and placed his crown made of hedgehog skins upon Cartier's head ; before bowing to the ground. The Indians regarded him as some kind of god and lost no time in bringing their sick to him to be touched and cured. Cartier made the sign of the cross over them.

. . . and opened a service book and read the passion of Christ in a loud voice during which all the natives kept a profound silence, looking up to heaven and imitating all our gestures. He then caused our trumpets and other musical instruments to be sounded, which made the natives very merry.

As the autumn was drawing on, Cartier could explore no further inland although he viewed the land to the east from the top of a neighbouring mountain, and admired the beauty of the valley which was to become the site for the city of Montreal, and noted the rapids in the river. Then, they returned the way they came without mishap.

space without a floor where they light their fire and live together as a large family. At night, the men retire to the above mentioned quarters with their wives and children. Furthermore, there are lofts in the upper part of their houses where they

THE SECOND VOYAGE OF JACQUES CARTIER IN 1536 | 127

On Monday, **11th October**, we arrived at the harbour of St. Croix (close to the mouth of the river Charles) where our ships were lying, and found that the officers and sailors who had stayed behind, had built a fort in front of the ships, enclosed on all sides with large wooden logs planted upright and in good state to defend us against the whole countryside.

Fort of St. Croix   detail from map opposite

They now studied the customs of the Canadian Indians as it was too late to return to France.

These people share almost everything they own. They go clothed in beasts' skins and rather miserably. In winter they wear leggings and moccasins made of skins, and in summer they go barefoot. They are by no means a hard working people and turn over the soil with short sticks of about half a sword in length. With these they hoe their corn which is as large as a pea. They also have considerable quantities of melons, cucumbers, pumpkins, and peas and beans of various colours unlike our own. While the ice and snow last, they catch a great number of wild animals such as fawns, stags and bears, hares, martens, foxes, otters and others. They eat their meat quite raw, merely smoking it, and the same with their fish.

These people live in wigwams and their only luxury is tobacco smoking. The women of this country work much harder than the men, both at fishing and at tilling the ground and other tasks.

In the month of December we received warning that the plague had broken out among the people of Stadacona (Indians to the North of Canada) to such an extent, that already, by their own confession, more than 50 persons were dead. Hearing this we forbade them to come either to the fort or about us. But even though we had driven them away, the sickness broke out amongst us accompanied by most marvellous and extraordinary symptoms; for some lost all their strength, their legs became swollen and inflamed while their sinews contracted and turned as black as coal. In other cases the legs were found blotched with purple coloured blood. Then the disease would mount to the hips, thighs, shoulders, arms and neck. All their mouths were so tainted that the gums rotted way down to the roots of the teeth, which nearly fell out. The disease spread among the three ships to such an extent that in the middle of February 1536 of the 110 men forming our company, there were not ten in good health so that no one could aid the other, which was a grievous sight considering the place where we were.

We were in great dread of the people of the country, lest they should become aware of our plight and helplessness. To hide the sickness, our Commander, whom God kept continually in good health, whenever they came near the fort, would go out and meet them with two or three men, either sick or well, whom he ordered to follow him outside. When these were beyond the enclosure, he would pretend to try to beat them, and shouting and throwing sticks, would drive them back on

Map of the St Lawrence drawn after Cartier's third voyage, 1541. The artist has drawn some of the colonists. Notice that south is at the top.

board the ships, indicating to the Indians by signs that he was making all his men work below decks, some at caulking, others at baking bread and at other tasks; and that it would not do to have them loafing about outside.

From the middle of **November 1535** until **Saturday, the 15th of April 1536,** we lay frozen up in the ice, which was more than two fathoms in thickness, while on shore there was more than four feet of snow so that it was higher than the bulwarks of our ships. This lasted until the date mentioned above with the result that all our beverages froze in their casks. All about the decks of the ships, below hatches and above there was ice to the

THE SECOND VOYAGE OF JACQUES CARTIER IN 1536 | 129

depth of four finger breadths. The whole river (the St. Lawrence) was frozen up to beyond Hochelaga. During this period 25 of the best and most able seamen we had all died of the aforementioned malady. At that time there was little hope of saving more than 40 others, while the whole of the rest were ill except three or four.

Fortunately, Cartier learnt of a native cure: the leaves and bark of the White Cedar tree were boiled and reduced to a medicine. However, he feared that the Indians had learned of the weakness of the Frenchmen and planned to seize them. Cartier lured chief Donnacona on board and captured him. Then he set sail for Newfoundland taking the chief with him so that he could tell the King of France about the wonders of the kingdom of Saguenay.

On 19th June, we set forth from Newfoundland and were favoured at sea with such good weather that we reached St. Malo on **16th July, 1536,** thanks be to God, whom we implore on bringing our voyage to an end, to give us His grace and His paradise hereafter. Amen.

Cartier made a third voyage in 1541. He searched for the mythical kingdom of Saguenay which the Indians told him was rich in precious stones. But he found nothing. He had hoped to start a colony, but the settlement failed and broke up. Cartier died in 1557. Nearly fifty years later in 1605, a group of French protestants tried to settle in Acadia (Nova Scotia). Samuel de Champlain succeeded in founding Quebec in 1608.

Suggestions for practical work

1. Draw or preferably make a model of Hochelaga and/or one of the longhouses. Use materials and methods as close to those described as possible.

2. Make a frieze showing the main episodes in Cartier's adventures.

Questions to consider

How did the Indians of Canada treat Cartier? What did they try to stop him doing?

Write a description of the Indians of Hochelaga under headings such as—homes, food, work, customs . . . . . .

What did Cartier hope and expect to find in Canada?

How near was the real Canada to his hopes?

Why do you think the first settlements failed to last?

Would you have been prepared to settle in Canada in the sixteenth century?

Discover what you can about the settlements that did succeed in the seventeenth century.

Adapted from *The Voyages of Jacques Cartier* by H. P. Biggar, (Publications of the Public Archives of Canada, 1924).

14 Henry Hudson's Last Voyage

An engraving of London from the south bank by Visscher, 1616.

Visscher's panorama of London. Guildhall Library, photo J. R. Freeman

The failure of Willoughby, Chancellor, and Jenkinson to discover a North-East passage started men looking for a North-West passage to China through America. Jacques Cartier and Martin Frobisher failed to discover it but Sir Humphrey Gilbert wrote 'A Discourse to prove a passage to the Northwest to Cathay and the East Indies'. He believed that a strait existed between 62° and 72° North and thought that it was possible to sail to Cathay with 'all Easterly winds and return with any westerly winds'.

Henry Hudson led four expeditions to the North-West. Abacuk Prickett, one of the crew of the ship *Discovery*, wrote this account of Hudson's last voyage.

We began our voyage for the N.W. Passage on the **14th of April 1610;** alongside the isle of Sheppey, our Master sent back Master Colbert to the owners with his letter. The next day we weighed anchor and stood out for Harwich where we stayed between 8th and 20th of April. From Harwich, we sailed along the coast till we came to the Isles of Orkney and sailed from thence to the Isles of Faroe, and from thence to Iceland where we met with foggy weather and heard the noise of waves breaking on the shore but saw not the land whereupon our Master anchored. Here, we were in a bay in the Southeast part of the land. We weighed anchor and stood along the coast. One day being calm, we began fishing and caught good store of fish such as Cod, Ling and Butt (a flat fish like a sole) with other sorts we knew not. The next day, we had a good gale of wind and came in sight of the Isles of Westmoney where the King of Denmark has a fortress. In our course we saw that famous hill, Mount Hekla, which cast out much fire, a sign of foul weather to come in a short time. We left Iceland astern of us until we came across a sea of pack ice; as soon as our Master saw it, he stood back for Iceland to find a harbour, which we did in the N.W. part called Derefer, where we killed a good number of fowls. From there we put to sea again but as both the wind and weather were against us, our Master stood back for the harbour but could not reach it; however we discovered another to the South, where on the shore we found a hot spring. Here, all our Englishmen bathed themselves; the water was so hot that it would scald a fowl for the pot.

On the 1st of June, we set sail for Greenland and saw what we thought to be land to the West; we bore towards it for the best part of a day, but it proved to be but a bank of fog, so we gave up and made for Greenland which we sighted on the 4th of June. A great amount of ice hung about its coast so that our Master could not reach the shore by any means. The land in this part is very mountainous and full of round hills like sugar loaves, covered with snow. We hugged the land as near as the ice would suffer us. Our course for the most part was between West and Northwest till we raised the 'Desolations' in the West part of Greenland. On this coast we saw a great many whales and at one time three of them came so close to us that we could hardly avoid them: two

passed very near and the third went under our ship; we received no harm from them, praise be God.

From the Desolations our Master made his way Northwest as the wind prevented him from going to the North; on this course we saw our first great Island or Mountain of ice; afterwards we were to see many more. About the latter end of June, we raised land to the West of us (Baffin Island) which our Master took to be that Island which Master Davis set down on his chart. On the West side of his Strait, our Master would have gone to the North but the wind would not suffer him to, so we sailed to the South of it into a strong rippling current which flowed to the West. Into this current, we went and made our way to the North-of-West till we met with the ice which hung about this Island. Our Master cast about until he cleared himself of this ice and then stood to the South and then to the West through a mass of floating ice upon which were many seals.

Hudson was making his way through what is now called Hudson's Strait into Hudson's Bay.

We gained a clear sea again and continued on our course till we met ice: first icebergs and then pack ice. Between them, we made our course Northwest till we met the ice again. In amongst the ice, we saw one of the great islands of ice overturn, which was a good warning to us not to come too close to them, nor within their reach. The next day, we had a storm and the wind brought the ice upon us so fast that in the end we were driven to put the ship into the middle of the ice and there let her lie. Some of our men, this day, fell sick, I will not say for fear although I saw little sign of any other sickness.

The North Pole

Hudson's Bay

James Bay

Hudson Strait

CANADA

Baffin Island

Baffin Bay

Davis Strait

The Desolations

GREENLAND

Newfoundland

Iceland

Arctic Circle

Mt. Hekla

Faroe Islands

Orkney Islands

Harwich
London

Route of Hudson's last voyage

HENRY HUDSON'S LAST VOYAGE | 133

The storm ceasing, we stood away from the ice into any clear sea we could find, which was sometimes more, sometimes less. Our course was the same as the ice although it was sometimes to the North, then to the Northwest, then to the West and to the Southwest, but still we were enclosed in ice. When our Master saw this, he set course to the South thinking to get clear of the ice that way, but the more he strove, the worse things got till we could go no further. Here our Master was in despair (as he told me afterwards) as he thought that he would never get out of this ice but would perish. Therefore he brought forth his chart and showed all the company that we had sailed a hundred leagues further west than any other Englishmen, and left it to their choice whether they would proceed any further: yea or nay. Whereupon, some were of one mind and some of another, some wishing themselves at home and some not caring where so long as they were out of the ice. After much labour and time spent, we gained room to turn our ship in, and so little by little got clear.

In the end we came in sight of land to the Southwest, high land covered with snow; our Master named this land 'Desire Provokes'. Lying here, we heard the noise of a great current of water coming out from the land. Being so well acquainted with the ice, when night, fog and foul weather came upon us, we would seek out the biggest island of ice and come to anchor there, and run and sport and fill our water casks from the ponds on the ice, which were both sweet and good. On this course we saw a bear upon a piece of ice by itself which our men chased in their boat, but before they could reach her, the tide had carried the ice and the bear on it into the pack so they wasted their labour and came aboard again.

Hudson continued his hunt for open water and gradually made his way further South. In this miserable atmosphere, bickering amongst the crew became dangerous and Hudson felt himself obliged to demote his mate and boatswain and to replace them with men he felt he could trust. His own judgement was at fault on occasions.

Out went our boat to the land that was next to us but it could not get close in to the shore as it was so shallow, yet ashore they got. Here, our men saw the footmarks of a man and a duck in the

snowy rocks and found plenty of wood, some of which they took and returned aboard. At midnight, we weighed anchor and stood to go out (of the bay) as we came in, and had not gone long before the carpenter came and told the Master that if he kept to his course he would be upon the rocks: the Master believed that he was past them when presently we ran on them and there stuck fast for 12 hours; by the mercy of God we got off unhurt, though not unscared.

Now, it was obvious that they were in the grip of winter and Hudson had to find a suitable place for them to live until the spring thaw. He chose a site somewhere on the shores of James Bay.

Here our Master sent out a boat with myself and the carpenter to seek a place to winter in; and it was time, for the nights were long and cold and the earth covered with snow. Having spent three months in a Labyrinth [he means that the ice-covered Hudson's Bay was like a maze] without

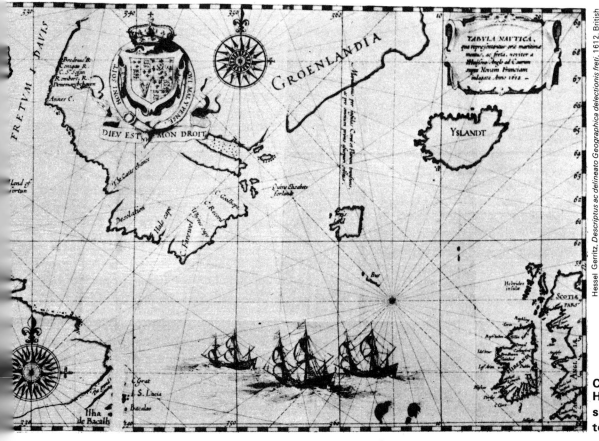

Chart made after Hudson's second voyage showing the approaches to Hudson Bay.

end, being now the last of October, we went down to the East to the bottom of the Bay. We found a place to which we brought our ship and pulled her out of the water: and this was the first of November. By the 10th thereof we were frozen in. We were provisioned for six months and had to share them in such a way that we could survive until such time as we could reach the Capes where the fowl bred (they had passed and noted these on their way South). For this reason, our Master made order for the use of what we had and for adding to it by offering rewards to them that killed either Beast, Fish or Fowl.

Now out of season and time, the Master called the carpenter to get on with a house on shore, which at the beginning our Master would not hear of when it might have been done. The carpenter told him that the snow and frost were such as he neither could nor would undertake such work. When our Master heard this, he ferreted him out of his cabin, struck him, called him by many foul names, and threatened to hang him. The carpenter told him that he knew what belonged to his place better than he, that he was no house carpenter. This passed and the house was made with much labour but to no purpose.

But I must not forget to show how mercifully God dealt with us in this time: for the space of three months, we had a great store of fowls: partridges as white as milk of which we killed more than 100 dozen, besides other birds of various sorts—for all were fish to our net. When the Spring came, the fowl left us and yet they were with us throughout the extreme cold. Then, in their place came various other birds such as swan, geese, duck and teal, but they were hard to come by. Then, we went out into the woods, hills and valleys to search for all things that had any substance in them however vile: the moss of the ground (than which I take the powder of a wooden post to be much better) and the frog were not spared. But amongst the different sorts of buds, it pleased God that Thomas Woodhouse brought home the bud of a tree full of turpentine substance. Of this our surgeon made a concoction to drink, and applied heated buds to the bodies of them that were troubled with aches. I for my own part received great and immediate easing of my pain.

About this time, when the ice began to break up and flow out of the Bays, there came a savage to our ship as it were to see and to be seen; he was the first we had seen in all this time. Our Master treated him well and made much of him hoping that great things might be done by means of him. He called for all the knives and hatchets which the crew had but received none except from John King, the carpenter, and myself. Our Master gave the savage a knife, a looking glass and buttons, he received them thankfully and made signs that after he had slept he would come again as he did. When he came, he brought with him a sledge which he pulled after him and upon it he had two deers' skins and two bears' skins.

Now (**May, 1611**), the ice being out of the Sounds (the small bays and channels) so that our boat might go from one place to another, a company of men were appointed by the Master to go fishing with our net. These men the first day they went caught 500 fish as big as good herrings and some trouts, which gave us some hope that our wants could be made good and our meal table improved.

The wind serving, we weighed anchor and sailed for home. On Monday night (**the 18th day of June**), we found ourselves in the ice and the next day, the wind being in the West we had to lay there in sight of land where we remained until Sunday. Being thus in the ice on Saturday (**the 21st of June**), at night, William Wilson the boatswain and Henry Green (one of Hudson's own friends) came to me in my cabin where I was lying lame, and told me that they and the rest of their associates would look after the company by turning the Master and all the sick men into the shallop (the ship's boat) and let them shift for themselves for there was not 14 days provisions left for all the crew. When I heard this, I told them that I marvelled to hear such things from them considering that they were married men and had wives and children and that for their sakes they should not commit so foul a crime in the sight of God and man. Henry Green bade me hold my peace for he knew the worst that could happen to him which was to be hanged at home, and of the two, he would rather be hanged at home than starved abroad.

In the meantime Henry Green and another went to the carpenter and held him in talk till the Master came out of his cabin when John Thomas and Bennett came before him and Wilson bound his arms behind him. He asked what they meant, they told him he should know when he was in the shallop. Then the shallop was drawn up to the ship's side and the poor sick and lame men were called upon to get them out of their cabins and into the shallop. The Master called to me, who came out of my cabin as well as I could, to the hatchway to speak with him; where on my knees I besought them for the love of God to remember themselves and to do as they would be done to. They bade me to look after myself and get me to my cabin not suffering the Master to speak with me.

What happened to Hudson, the sickmen and his son Jack who insisted on staying with his father we do not know. The mutineers endured great hardships: five of them including Henry Green, the ringleader of the mutiny, were killed in a fight with some Eskimoes while the rest (one officer, Robert Bylot, and seven men) were reduced to eating 'fowls' and candles the latter being regarded as a great 'dainty'—each man was allowed a pound of candles a week. The crew became 'so weak that they could not stand at the helm but were forced to sit'. Finally they reached the west coast of Ireland and made their way back to England where they were imprisoned, but were released after a short time presumably because they had suffered enough.

The Mutineers took home Hudson's journals and charts which were studied by the officials of Trinity House; the crew was also closely cross-questioned about their discoveries. As a result of this investigation, it was decided that the evidence provided by the currents flowing from East to West proved that a Passage did exist, and so more expeditions were sent until William Baffin reported in 1616 'there is no passage, nor hope of passage in the North of Davis Straits, we have coasted all or near all the circumference thereof, and find it to be no other than a great Bay'.

In 1969, a giant ice-breaking tanker, the SS. *Manhattan*, fulfilled the 500 year old dream by smashing its way through the ice from Eastern Canada to Alaska.

Adapted from Abacuk Prickett's Account of 'Hudson's Last Voyage' printed in *Samuel Purchas' Divers Voyages and Northern Discoveries of 1612*.

There are no contemporary drawings or prints of Hudson's last voyage. Why do you think this is so? You might draw your own illustrations of some of the episodes.

Questions to consider

What was the most frightening time during this voyage? Why did Hudson sail southwards when he was in his bay? Was he disappointed in his hopes?

Why did Hudson quarrel with his carpenter? What effect do you think this incident had upon the rest of the crew?

Why did the men grow discontented during the voyage?

How far do you feel that Hudson was responsible? Why do you think that Prickett was allowed to stay on board? Do you accept his version of what happened?

Compare the voyages of Barents and Hudson. Why do you think there was such a difference?

15 Jenkinson's Russian Journey

In the second half of the sixteenth century, English merchants were searching for new markets for their goods. The northern shores of Europe and Russia seemed to offer such trading opportunities. There was another reason for exploring the northern seas: many people believed that it was possible to sail right across the Arctic Sea to China itself.

In 1553 the Muscovy Company was set up 'for the discovery of regions, dominions, islands and places unknown'. The first voyage financed by the company was commanded by Sir Hugh Willoughby and Richard Chancellor. Their ships were parted by a storm and Willoughby and all his crew died of cold in Lapland. Chancellor reached the White Sea, and made his way overland to Moscow. The Tsar of the Russians received him and was glad to open trade with England.

The Company chose Anthony Jenkinson to lead a fleet to Russia and to seek another meeting with the Tsar. The Company hoped that the Tsar might allow Jenkinson to travel across Russia to trade with the peoples in the East. The following account is based on Jenkinson's own journal.

First by the grace of God, the **12th day of May, 1557**, I departed from London and the same day at Gravesend embarked myself in a good ship named the *Primrose*, being appointed although unworthy chief captain of the same and also three other good ships, having also to conduct the Emperor of Russia's ambassador, Joseph Nepea, in the said *Primrose*. And our four tall ships being well appointed for men and victuals* as other

* Foodstuffs.

necessary furniture, we weighed our anchors and departed from Gravesend. Plying down the Thames, the wind being Easterly and fair weather, the 13th day we came aground with the *Primrose* upon a sandbank called 'the Blacktail', where we sat fast until the 14th in the morning and then God be praised she came off.

Thus continuing our course along the coast of Norway, the 27th day we took the sun (with an astrolabe) and found that we had reached latitude 69°. In the same day in the afternoon appeared over head a rainbow like a semi-circle with both ends upward. Note that there is between the Rest Islands and Lofoten, a whirlpool called Maelstrom which from half ebb until half flood maketh such a terrible noise that it shaketh the rings in the doors of the inhabitants' houses on the islands ten miles off. Also if any whales cometh within the current of the same, they make a pitiful cry. Note that the 6th day (of July) we passed by the place where Sir Hugh Willoughby and all his company perished.

They were now coasting along the shores of Lapland:

The land of Lappia is a high land having snow lying on it commonly all the year. The people of this country are heathens; they live in the summer time near the seaside and catch fish of which they make bread; and in the winter they move up country into the woods where they hunt and kill deer, bears, wolves, foxes and other beasts with whose flesh they are nourished and with whose skins they are clothed in such strange fashion that there is nothing seen of them bare but their eyes.

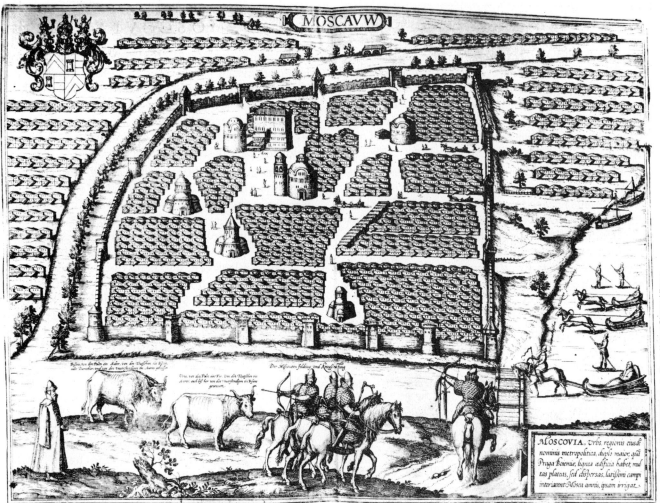

Moscow in 1573

They have no other habitations but tents, moving from place to place according to the season of the year. They know no art nor skill but shooting which they exercise daily, women as well as men, and kill such beasts as serve them for their food.

The 12th day of July, all our four ships arrived safely at the harbour of St. Nicholas in the land of Russia where we anchored; we had sailed 750 leagues. The Russian ambassador with great joy went ashore, and our ships forthwith discharged themselves, and on being laden again and having a fair wind, departed toward England on the **1st of August**. The 3rd of the said month, I with my company came unto the city of Kholmogori being 100 verts (a vert measures 3,500 feet) from the bay of St. Nicholas.

They travelled by river to Vologda where Jenkinson described the houses.

The houses are built with the wood of fir trees, made into round logs and joined together. The houses are squares without any iron or stone work and are covered with Birch bark and wood. Their churches are all of wood, two to every parish: one to be heated for winter and the other for summer. On top of their houses they lay much earth for fear of burning for they are plagued with fires.

They quickly covered the 500 versts to Moscow by sled.

Moscow

The city of Moscow is great; though the houses are for the most part of wood, some are of stone, with windows of iron which serve for summer time. There are many fair churches of stone, but more of wood, which are heated in winter time. The Emperor's lodging is a fair sized kremlin-castle, a square of high, thick brick walls situated upon a hill with the rivers on the Southwest side of it; it hath 16 gates in the walls and as many ramparts. His palace is separated from the rest of the castle by a long roadway down to the river side. In his palace are churches, some of stone and some of wood with beautifully gilded round towers. In the church doorways and within the churches are golden images. The chief markets for all things are within the castle; there is a market for each kind of product. Also in the winter, the river being frozen, there is a great market outside the castle's walls on the ice where corn, earthenware pots, sleds and so on are sold.

The Emperor's name in their tongue is Ivan Vasilivich. Before his father, they were neither called emperors nor kings but only grand dukes. This Emperor uses great familiarity as well with all his nobles and subjects as also with strangers who serve him either in his wars or in other

Ivan Vasilivich—the Terrible

occupations; for his pleasure is that they shall dine oftentimes in the year in his presence. By this means he is not only beloved of his nobles and common people but also held in great dread and fear through all his dominions, so that I think no prince in Christendom is more feared for himself than he is, nor yet better loved. His Majesty hears all complaints himself and with his own mouth gives sentence and judgment on all matters speedily. He delighteth not greatly in hawking, hunting or any pastime, nor in hearing instruments and music, but setteth his whole delight upon two things: first to serve God as undoubtedly he is very devout in his religion, and second to subdue and conquer his enemies.

On the 10th day of December, I was sent for by the said Emperor and delivered my letters unto the secretary. The 25th day, being the day of the Nativity, I came into the Emperor's presence and kissed his hand, who sat aloft in a goodly chair of state, having on his head a richly jewelled crown and a staff of gold in his hand, and being apparelled in cloth of gold garnished with precious stones. And after I had done obeisance to the Emperor, he with his own mouth calling me by name bade me come to dinner, and so I departed to my lodging till dinner time which was at 6 o'clock by candle light. The Emperor dined in a fair great hall in the midst whereof was a four sided pillar very cleverly made, about which were several tables set. At the uppermost part of the hall sat the Emperor himself; I was sat at a little table directly before the Emperor's face. The Emperor sent me various bowls of wine and mead and many dishes of meat from his own hand, which were brought me by a duke, and my table was served with gold and silver and so were the other tables likewise.

The Tartars
Jenkinson obtained the Tsar's permission to travel beyond his lands in search of trade.

The 23rd day of April, 1558, I departed from Moscow by water, having with me two of your servants (the (Muscovy Company's), namely Richard Johnson and Robert Johnson and a Tartar called Tolmach with various parcels of our wares.

Very soon, he reached Kazan, where he stayed for over a month before pushing on to Astrakhan. These were the ancient cities of the Mongols.

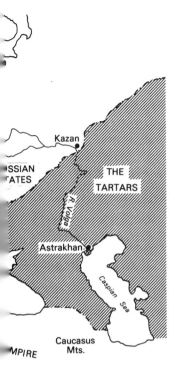

Tartar warrior

Thevenot Relation de Divers Voyages curieux, 1663. Bodleian Library

The Tartars or Mongols were originally nomadic herders on the great Steppes, but then Ghengis Khan made them into a great warrior nation and they invaded Russia in 1223. They settled down on the plains around the river Volga, along the northern shores of the Black Sea and in Siberia and forced the Russians to pay tribute for hundreds of years. Their power declined during the fifteenth century. Ivan the Terrible was able to defeat them and capture their great cities, Kazan in 1552 and Astrakhan in 1556—just a few years before Jenkinson's journey. Jenkinson was horrified by the conditions he saw.

And at my being at the said Astrakhan, there was a great famine and plague among the people and especially among the Tartars who came thither in great numbers to render homage to the Russians their enemies, and to seek succour at their hands, the country being destroyed; but they were ill entertained or relieved for there died a great number of them for hunger, and lay in heaps throughout all the islands, like beasts unburied, very pitiful to behold. Many of them were sold by the Russians and the rest were banished from the island. At that time it would have been an easy thing to have converted that wicked nation to the Christian faith, if the Russians had been good Christians; but how could they show compassion unto other nations when they are not merciful unto their own.

We entered into the Caspian Sea on the 10th day of August at the Easterly side of the river Volga.

After suffering from storms and contrary winds, Jenkinson had an alarming experience.

Being at anchor opposite this river Iac and all our men being on land, saving I who lay sore sick and five Tartars, one of whom was reputed to be a holy man (because he came from Mecca), there came a boat unto us with 30 men well armed and appointed, who boarded us. Our holy Tartar called Azy asked them what they would have and started to pray. With that these rovers declared that they were gentlemen banished from their country and came to see if there were any Russians or other Christians in our bark. Azy most stoutly answered that there were none, vowing the same by great oaths which the rovers believed and upon his words departed. And so through the loyalty of that Tartar, I with all my company and goods were saved; and our men being come on board and the wind fair, we departed from that place; that day being the 20th of August.

At length, after more storms, they landed on the eastern shores of the Caspian Sea and joined a caravan of 1,000 camels. After riding for some time, they were stopped by Tartars.

They stopped our caravan in the name of their Prince and opened our wares, and took such things as they thought best for their Prince without paying for them. I rode to the Prince and presented myself to him, requesting his favour and a passport to travel through his country: which request he granted me and entertained me, commanding me to be well feasted with flesh and mare's milk: for bread they have none, nor other drink except water. He had no money for the things he took from me, but gave me his letter (of safe conduct) and a horse worth seven roubles. This Sultan lived in the fields without a castle or a town in a little round house made of reeds covered with felt. So having permission, I departed and overtook our caravan and proceeded on our journey. We travelled for 20 days in the wilderness without seeing town or habitation, and were driven of necessity to eat one of my camels and a horse. During the said 20 days we found no water, but such as we drew out of old deep wells, being very brackish and salt, and yet sometimes we passed two or three days without even that.

On the 5th day of October, we came again to a gulf of the Caspian Sea where we found very fresh and sweet water. We, having refreshed ourselves at the gulf, departed thence and the 7th day arrived at a castle called Sellizure where the king is called Azim Khan. I was commanded to come before his presence and delivered the Emperor of Russia's letters; I also gave him a present of a ninth (of our wares); he entertained me well and gave me letters of safe conduct on my departure.

The castle of Sellizure is situated upon an high hill where the king called the Khan lieth, the palace is built of earth and is not very strong; the people are but poor and have little merchandise to trade. The water that serves all that country is drawn by ditches out of the river Oxus.

This is the land of the Tartars, who live without town or habitation in the wild fields, removing from one place to another in great companies with their cattle of which they have a large number, as well as camels, horses and sheep both tame and wild. There are many wild horses which the Tartars do often kill with their hawks. The Tartars never ride without their bow, arrows and sword even though they may be hawking or at any other pleasure; they are good archers both on horseback and on foot. Bread they have none for they neither till nor sow; they be great devourers of meat, which they cut in small pieces and eat by handfuls most greedily, especially horseflesh. Their chief drink is soured milk and they become drunk with the same. Use of money have they none, but do barter their cattle for apparel and other necessaries. They delight in no art or science except the wars wherein they are expert, but for the most part they are pasturing people.

They passed through the town of Urgench, and found themselves in an area terrorised by bands of robbers:

Certain Tartars of our company called holy men (because they had been to Mecca) wanted the whole caravan to stop so that they could make their prayers to discover how we should prosper in our journey and whether we should meet with any ill company or no; to which our whole caravan did agree, so they took certain sheep and killed them and took their shoulderblades, burnt them, took the blood of the sheep and mingled it with the

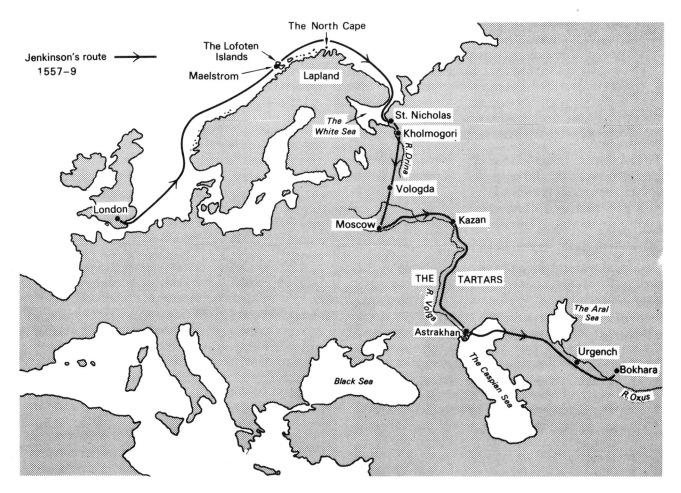

Jenkinson's route ⟶
1557–9

The North Cape

The Lofoten
Islands

Maelstrom

Lapland

The
White Sea

St. Nicholas

Kholmogori

R. Drina

Vologda

Moscow

Kazan

THE   TARTARS

R. Volga

Astrakhan

The Aral
Sea

Urgench

Bokhara

R. Oxus

The Caspian Sea

Black Sea

London

powder of the bones and wrote with the mixture certain signs and letters. Using many other ceremonies and words, by the same they devined that we should meet with enemies and thieves to our great trouble but should overcome them; to which sorcery, I and my company gave no credit, but we found it to be true, for within three hours, we saw afar off some horsemen who made for us so we gathered ourselves together, being 40 of us well appointed and able to fight. When the thieves were near unto us, we perceived them to be 37 in number, men well armed and appointed with bows, arrows and swords. They wished us to yield ourselves or else be slain, but we defied them. With that they shot at us and we at them very hotly, and so continued our fight from morning until two hours after dark; several men, horses and camels were slain on both sides. Had it not been for four handguns which I and my company had and used, we would have been overcome and destroyed.

The next morning, the thieves allowed themselves to be bought off and the caravan made its way:

To the river Oxus, where we refreshed ourselves, having been three days without water and drink and tarried there all the next day, making merry with our slain horses and camels.

After further hardships in the wilderness, the caravan reached Bokhara on 23 December:

This Bokhara is situated in the lowest part of the land and is walled about with a high wall of earth with several gates in the same; it is divided into three parts: two are the king's and the third is the merchants' and every craft has its own street and market. The city is very great and the houses for the most part are made of earth, but there are also many houses, temples and monuments sumptuously built of stone and richly decorated especially the bathhouses, the like of which is not to be found in the world. There is yearly great resort of merchants to this city who travel in great caravans from countries such as India, Persia, Russia and many others. The Indians bring fine white cottons which the Tartars bind around their heads, but gold, silver, precious stones and spices bring they none. I enquired and learned that all such trade passes to the Indian Ocean and that the markets where all such things are to be had are in subjection to the Portuguese. I offered to barter with merchants of these countries, but they would not trade for such a commodity as our cloth.

Because of the wars between the Tartars and the Persians, Jenkinson had to return to Moscow. The Muscovy Company flourished and trade was started with Persia and Turkey. Jenkinson had a successful career and visited Russia on several occasions.

Adapted from *The Principal Navigations, Voyages, Traffiques and Discoveries of the English Nation* by Richard Hakluyt, (Dent).

Suggestions for practical work

1. Make a model of a Russian log house.
2. Write an illustrated account of the way of life of either the Lapps or the Tartars.
3. Write a description of sixteenth-century Moscow or Bokhara.

Questions to consider

Why did Jenkinson travel to Russia?

Look up Ivan the Terrible and write an account of his life. Does Jenkinson's description agree with that of historians?

Why do you think the Russians treated the Tartars so badly?

What were Jenkinson's main difficulties in his journey through the land of the Tartars?

Why were the eastern merchants reluctant to trade with the English?

Which part of the journey do you imagine he enjoyed most?

16 The Voyages of William Barents

De Bry, *Voyages*, c. 1600. Bodleian Library

This engraving and the others in the pamphlet were made to illustrate a book about Barents' journey by one of the crew.

William Barents' chart of the Arctic regions, published in 1599.

Early in the sixteenth century, men had started to argue that ships could pass through the ice of the Arctic Sea to China. Robert Thorne, a London merchant, wrote to Henry VIII asking him to finance such an enterprise.

To which places (China and the Spice Islands) there is left one way to discover, which is unto the North . . . it is clear and certain that those seas be navigable and without any danger, but that ships may pass and have in them perpetual clearness of the day without any darkness of the night ... For being past this little way which they thought so dangerous (which may be two or three leagues before they come to the Pole, and as much more after they pass the Pole) it is clear, that from thenceforth the sea and lands are as temperate as in these parts ... If they go towards the Orient, they shall enjoy the region of all the Tartars that extend towards the midday, and from thence they may go and proceed to the lands of the Chinas ... And if from thence they do continue their navigation, following the coasts that return toward the Occident, they shall fall in with Malacca ... and following the way, may return hither by the Cape of Good Hope; and thus they shall compass the whole world.

Merchants and sailors in Europe thought that this description was correct and voyages were made to find the North-East Passage. In the nineties of the sixteenth century, the merchants of Amsterdam took up the search and three expeditions (1594, 1595, and 1596/7) under William Barents sailed to the North East. William Barents was pilot of the third expedition under the command of Jacob van Heemskerk.

Route of Barents' last journey ⟶

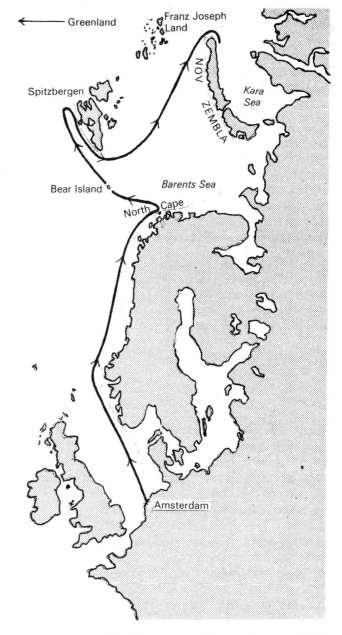

A lively account of these voyages was written by Gerrit de Veer, a Dutchman; and the following extracts were taken from his description of their third expedition.
They sailed from Amsterdam on 10th May 1596.
By the 1st June, they had reached a latitude where there was no night.

The 5th June, we saw the first ice, which we wondered at, at first thinking that it had been white swans for one of our men walking in the foredeck on a sudden began to cry out with a loud voice, saying that he saw white swans, at which we that were below decks immediately came up, and perceived that it was ice that came driving from the great ice packs; at midnight we sailed through it.

Sighting the North Cape of Lapland, they followed a north-westerly course until on 9th June they reached an island. A landing party nearly perished, as having climbed a steep snow mountain, they found it difficult to descend.

We thought we should all have broken our necks, it was so slippery, but we sat upon the snow and slid down, which was very dangerous for us, for at the foot of the hill there were many rocks.

The 12th of June in the morning we saw a white bear which we rowed after with our boat, thinking to cast a rope around her neck, but when we were near her, she was so great that we dared not do it, but rowed back again to our ships to fetch more men and our arms, and so made to her again with muskets, arquebuses, halberds and hatchets, John Cornellyson's men coming also with their boat to help us. And so being well furnished of men and weapons, we rowed with both our boats unto the bear, and fought with her while four glasses were run out (2 hours) for our weapons could do her

little hurt; and amongst the rest of the blows that we gave her, one of our men struck her in the back with an axe, which stuck fast in her, and yet she swam away with it, but we rowed after her, and at last we cut her head in sunder with an axe, wherewith she died and we brought her into John Cornellyson's ship where we flayed her and found her skin to be twelve feet long: which done we ate some of her flesh but it did not agree with us. This island we called the Bear Island.

The 19th June we saw land again . . . It is here also to be noted that in this land which we believe to be Greenland (in fact it was Spitzbergen), lying under 80° and more, there groweth leaves and grass, and there are such beasts therein as eat grass such as harts, bucks and such like beasts, yet in Nova Zembla which lieth under 76°, there groweth neither leaves nor grass, nor any beasts that eat grass or leaves, but only such beasts as eat flesh, like bears and foxes, and yet this land lieth full 4° (further) from the North Pole.

On 23rd June . . . our men went on land to see how much the needle of the compass varied. Meantime, there came a great white bear swimming towards the ship and would have climbed up into it if we had not made a noise and shot at her with a piece, but she left the ship and swam to land . . . Touching the varying of the compass, for the which cause our men went on land to try the certainty thereof, it was found to differ 16°.

The 16th August ten of our men entering into one boat rowed to the firm land of Nova Zembla and drew the boat up upon the ice, which done, we went up a high hill to see the situation of the land and found that it reached S.E. and S.S.E. and then again South which we disliked, for that it lay so much southward: but when we saw open water S.E. and E.S.E. of us we were much comforted again, thinking that we had won our prize (offered by the Dutch Estates-General or Parliament for the discovery of the N.E. Passage) and knew not how we should get soon enough on board to certify William Barents thereof.

They sailed on, rounded the northern end of Nova Zembla and unexpectedly found themselves in a good harbour, but:

The next day, 24th August, it blew hard N.N.W. and the ice came mightily driving in whereby we were in a manner compassed about therewith. Moreover the wind began more and more to rise, and the ice still pressed harder and harder, so that the pin of the rudder and the rudder itself were shorn in pieces, and our boat was torn to pieces between the ship and the ice, we expected nothing else but that the ship also would be pressed and crushed in pieces by the ice . . . the ice came up with great force under the bow and lifted the ship

De Bry. *Voyages.* c.1600. Bodleian Library

up four foot high above it so that it seemed that the ship would be overthrown in the place, whereupon they that were in the ship put out the boat therewith to save their lives.

On the 28th August we got some of the ice from it and the ship began to sit upright again, but before it was fully upright, as William Barents and the other pilot went forward to the bow to see how the ship lay and how much it was risen, and while they were busy upon their knees and elbows to measure how much it was, the ship burst out of the ice with such a noise and so great a crack, that they verily thought they were all cast away, knowing not how to save themselves.

The 29th August, the ship lying upright again, we used all the means we could with iron hooks (crowbars) and other instruments to break the flakes of ice that lay one heaped upon the other, but all in vain; so we determined to commit ourselves to the mercy of God.

De Bry, *Voyages*. c.1600. Bodleian Library

On 5th September we took counsel together and carried our old sock sail (foresail) with powder, lead, pieces, muskets and other furniture on to the land to make a tent about our boat we had drawn upon the land, and at the same time we carried ashore some bread and wine also some timber, with which to mend our boat that it might serve us in time of need . . . we took counsel together (11th September) what to do for the best in the circumstances of the time in order that we might winter here and attend such adventure as God would send us: and after we had debated upon the matter, we determined to build a shed or house upon land to keep and defend ourselves both from the cold and the wild animals. And to that end we went further into the land to find out the convenientest place in our opinions to raise our house upon.

The 26th September we had a wet wind and an open sea, but our ship lay fast wherewith we were not a little grieved, but it was God's will which

De Bry, *Voyages*, c.1600. Bodleian Library

we most patiently bore, and we began to make our house: part of our men fetched wood to burn, the rest played the carpenter and were busy about the house. There were 16 men in all for our carpenter was dead.

The 27th September it blew hard N.E., and it froze so hard that as we put a nail into our mouths (like men who do carpenter's work do) ice would hang thereon when we took it out again, and make the blood follow. The same day there came an old bear and a young one towards us as we were going to our house, being altogether (for we durst not go alone), which we thought to shoot at, but they ran away. At which time the ice came driving in with great force, and it was fair sunshine weather, but so extreme cold that we could hardly work, but extremity forced us thereunto.

Barents and the crew settled down to endure a 'cold, comfortless, dark and dreadful Winter'.

THE VOYAGES OF WILLIAM BARENTS | 153

Hut where the crew spent the winter of 1596-7. Notice the bath made out of a barrel, with the ship's clock hung above, the hour glass on the table on the left and the oil lamp.

De Bry, *Voyages*, c.1600, Bodleian Library

The 27th October the wind blew N.E. and it snowed so fast that we could not work without the door. That day our men killed a white fox, which they flayed, and after they had roasted it, ate thereof, which tasted like connies' (rabbits') flesh. The same day we set up our clock and made it strike and we hung up a lamp to burn in the night time, wherein we used the fat of the bear, which we melted and burnt in the lamp.

The 4th November it was calm weather, but then we saw the sun no more for it was no longer above the horizon. Then our surgeon made us a bath to bathe us in, out of a pipe* of wine wherein we entered one after another, and it did us much good and was a great means of our health.

The 8th November the same day we shared our bread amongst us, each man having four pounds ten ounces as his allowance for 8 days; so that we were 8 days eating a barrel of bread, whereas before we ate it up in 5 or 6 days.

The 12th November That day we began to share our wine, every man had 2 glasses a day, but commonly our drink was water which we melted out of snow which gathered without the house.

The 20th November we washed our sheets, but it was so cold that when we had washed and wrung them, they immediately froze so stiff that although we laid them by a great fire, the side that lay next the fire thawed but the other side was hard frozen.

The 2nd December it was still foul weather whereby we were forced to keep within the house,

* A pipe was a barrel of wine.

and yet we could hardly sit by the fire because of the smoke and therefor stayed still in our cots; and then we heated stones, which we put into our cots to warm our feet.

The 7th December heat being so great a comfort to us, we took care to make it continue long: whereupon we agreed to stop up all the doors and the chimney thereby to keep in the heat, and so went into our cots to sleep . . . but at last we were taken with a great swooning and dizziness in our heads which was first perceived by a sick man who was therefor less able to bear it, and we soon found ourselves to be very ill at ease, so that some of us that were strongest started out of our beds and first opened the chimney and then the doors . . . And when the doors were open, we all recovered our health again . . .

The 25th December, being Christmas Day, it was foul weather . . . we heard the foxes run over our house, wherewith some of our men said it was an ill sign; and while we sat disputing why it should be an ill sign, one of our men made answer that it was an ill sign because we could not take them to put them into the pot to roast them, for that had been a very good sign to us.

And when we had toiled all day, we remembered ourselves that it was Three Kings' Even (5th January), and then we prayed our master that we might be merry that night, and said we were content to drink some of the wine that night . . . so that we made merry and drank to the Three Kings.

The 16th January it was fair weather, the wind northerly; and we went now and then out of the house to stretch our joints and our limbs with walking, throwing the ball and running that we might not become lame; and about noon time we saw a certain redness in the sky, as a sign or messager of the sun that began to come towards us.

The weather continued to improve but the ice showed no sign of retreating from around the ship so the crew became impatient to be off:

The 9th May it was fair clear weather with an indifferent wind out of the N.E.; at which time the desire that our men had to be gone from thence still more and more increased and then they agreed to speak to William Barents to move the Master (Jacob van Heemskerk) to go from thence, but he put them off with fair words.

The 29th May we took heart again and determined to turn the boat that lay by the house with her keel upwards, and we began to mend it (and to heighten the gunwhales) so that it might be the fitter to carry us over the sea.

Re-building the ship's boat for the return journey

De Bry, *Voyages*, c 1600, Bodleian Library

The 13th June. And so having finished all things as we determined, we drew the yawl to the water side (they had managed to preserve this during the winter as well), and went and fetched the boat. We went to the house and first drew William Barents up on a sledge to the place where our boats lay and after that we fetched Claus Adrianson, both of them having been long sick. And so we entered into the boats committing ourselves to the will and mercy of God, with a W.N.W. wind and indifferent open water, we set sail and put to sea.

The 17th June in the morning, when we had broken our fasts, the ice came so fast upon us that it made our hairs stand upright upon our heads, it was so fearful to behold, so that we thought verily that it was a foreshadowing of our last end. At last, being in this discomfort and extreme necessity, the Master said if we could but fasten a rope to the firm ice, we might therewith draw the boat

Loading up the boat for the voyage home. The ship was abandoned in the ice.

De Bry. *Voyages.* c.1600. Bodleian Library

up. I being the lightest of all our company took on the task of tying a rope upon the firm ice; and by creeping from one piece of drifting ice to another, by God's help, got to the firm ice, where I made a rope fast to a high hummock and they that were in the boat drew it thereby unto the said firm ice.

The 20th June we sat talking one with another, and spake of many things, and William Barents looked at my little chart which I had made of our voyage; at last he laid aside the chart and spake unto me saying 'Gerrit give me some drink' but he was taken with so sudden a qualm that he turned his eyes in his head and died immediately, and we had no time to call the Master out of the boat to speak unto him . . . The death of William Barents put us in no small discomfort being the chief guide and only pilot to whom we trusted ourselves next under God.

At last, after further adventures, the twelve survivors reached Amsterdam on 1 November 1597: they had been given up for dead many months before. In 1871, Barents' winter quarters were found on Nova Zembla.

There stood the cooking-pans over the fireplace, the old clocks against the wall, the arms, the tools, the drinking vessels, the instruments and the books that had beguiled the weary hours of that long night, two hundred and seventy-eight years ago.

Adapted from Gerrit de Veer, *Barents Three Voyages to the Arctic Regions*, ed. Charles T. Beke (Hakluyt Society).

Questions to consider

Where was Barents hoping to sail to?

Study the pictures and describe the landscape of Nova Zembla where the Dutch ships got stuck in the ice.

How did the sailors make their stores last out the winter?

How did they keep themselves healthy?

Pretend to be a member of Barents' crew and write a diary describing your life during the winter.

Why do you think the crew's morale remained high during their ten months' stay in Nova Zembla?

Write an epitaph or funeral speech for Barents.

Read Chapter 14 and see how Hudson's crew behaved in similar circumstances. Why do you think they reacted so differently?

17 The Adventures of Pinto in China and Japan

After Vasco da Gama's voyage to Calicut, the Portuguese established their control over the Indian Ocean by defeating the Arabs and the Ottoman Turks. Then, led by their great Viceroy, Alfonso d' Albuquerque, they attacked and seized the city of Malacca (1511) which was the western terminus of the Chinese fleets, gaining complete command of the spice trade. In 1513, the Portuguese reached Canton where the Chinese regarded the 'foreign devils' with contempt refusing to grant them special privileges. One of the most daring of the Portuguese adventurers in the Far East was Ferdinand Mendes Pinto (1509–83) who went out to Malacca in 1537 and returned to Portugal in 1558. During his retirement, he wrote a long account of his adventures called his 'Peregination' for his children. The following extract deals with a journey which started at Malacca in 1540 and ended there in 1544.

Voyage to China

We entered into a strait named Xalingau, much less frequented than the Gulf of Nanking, which in that place was not above ten or eleven leagues broad. We sailed for the space of thirteen days from one side to another with a westerly wind, exceedingly afflicted both by the great labour we were put to and the cruel fear we were in, besides we began to feel the want of victuals. Having come within sight of the mountains of Conxinacau, there arose so terrible a south wind, called by the Chinese a typhoon, that our vessels being low-built, weak and lacking mariners were put in danger, and so without hope of escape, we suffered ourselves to be driven along the coast with the current judging it better to venture among the rocks than to be swallowed up in the midst of the sea. Though we had chosen the less painful course, it did not succeed, for after dinner the wind turned to the north-west and the waves became so high that they were dreadful to behold; our fear was so extreme that we began to cast all that we had into the sea, even the chests of silver. That done, we cut down our two masts and so floated along all the rest of the day; at about midnight, we heard them in the other vessel cry: 'Lord, have mercy upon us,' which persuaded us that they were cast away, the knowledge of which put us in such a fright that for an hour no man spake a word. Having passed this sad night in so miserable a plight, about an hour before day our vessel opened about the keel, so that it was instantly full of water eight spans high. As soon as it was day, we looked out to sea but could not sight the other vessel. About ten of the clock the waves rolled us towards a point of rocks that stood out to sea, where no sooner had we arrived than all went to pieces; of the 25 Portuguese, there were but fourteen saved, the other eleven being drowned together with eighteen Christian servants and seven Chinese sailors. This miserable disaster happened on **Monday, the 5th of August, 1542.**

We fourteen Portugals, having escaped out of this shipwreck by the mercy of God, spent all that day and the night following in bewailing our misfortune, but in the end consulting together, we decided to enter the country hoping that we should not fail to meet with somebody who would relieve us with meat till such time as it would please heaven to terminate our travels with the end of our lives. We found upon the shore the

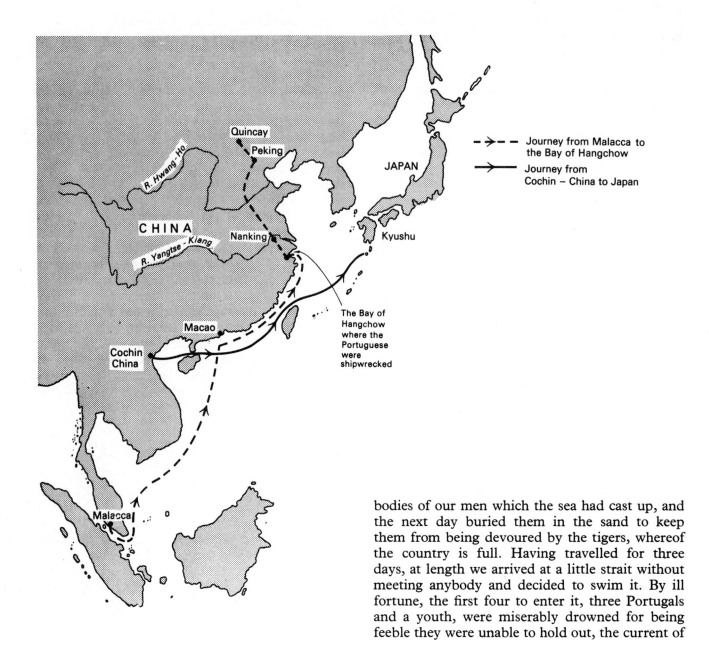

Journey from Malacca to the Bay of Hangchow

Journey from Cochin – China to Japan

Quincay

Peking

JAPAN

R. Hwang - Ho

CHINA

Nanking

Kyushu

R. Yangtse - Kiang

The Bay of Hangchow where the Portuguese were shipwrecked

Macao

Cochin China

Malacca

bodies of our men which the sea had cast up, and the next day buried them in the sand to keep them from being devoured by the tigers, whereof the country is full. Having travelled for three days, at length we arrived at a little strait without meeting anybody and decided to swim it. By ill fortune, the first four to enter it, three Portugals and a youth, were miserably drowned for being feeble they were unable to hold out, the current of the water being very strong and the strait somewhat broad. Having spent all that dark night exposed to the wind, rain and cold, we discovered a great fire towards the east whereupon we marched that way. At last, we came to a little wood, where we found five men making a fire of coals. We fell to eating the rice they gave us and then went directly to a hospital they told us of.

Here they were treated kindly and then begged their way from town to town.

Ill fortune brought us to a town called Taipor where by chance there was a Chumbin, that is one of those superintendants of justice that are sent out into the provinces to report to the Emperor of all that passeth there. This wicked man, seeing us begging from door to door, called to us from a window and would know who we were and of what nation. We answered him that we were strangers, natives of the Kingdom of Siam. Our answer satisfied the Chumbin and he would have let us go, had it not been for one of his clerks who told him that we were idle vagabonds. Then, he caused us to be put into a deep dungeon with irons on our hands and feet and great iron collars around our necks. In this miserable place, we endured such hunger and were so fearfully whipped that we were in perpetual pain for twenty days together. At the end thereof we were sent to the court of the Cheam of Nanking because the Chumbin did not have the power to put us to death.

After careful consideration of the evidence, the Cheam decided to send them on to Peking where the highest court in the land could deal with them. However, during the lengthy court proceedings, Mendes Pinto was able to study the town of Nanking.

Chinese peasants ploughing

A Mandarin in a sedan chair

Nanking

The city of Nanking is seated by the river Yangtse-Kiang upon a reasonably high hill so that it commands all the plains about it: the climate is somewhat cold but healthy. It is eight leagues in circumference; the houses in it are not above two storeys high and are all built of wood; only those of the mandarins (the Chinese government officials) are made of hewed stone, and surrounded with walls and ditches over which are stone bridges leading to gates with rich and costly decoration. The houses of the high officials are stately towers, six or seven storeys high and gilded all over; wherein they have gunpowder magazines, wardrobes, treasuries and a world of rich household stuff such as a mass of delicate and most fine porcelain, which amongst them is prized and esteemed as much as precious stones.

The Chinese assured us that in this city there are 800,000 fires, 80,000 mandarin's houses, 62 great market places, 130 butchers' shambles and 8,000 streets, we were further assured that there are likewise 2,300 pagodas (tall, tower-like-temples), 1,000 of which were monasteries of religious persons, whose buildings were exceeding rich and sumptuous with very high steeples wherein there were between 60 and 70 mighty huge bells—it was a dreadful thing to hear them rung. There are moreover 30 great strong prisons in the city, and each has 3 or 4,000 prisoners. At the entrance into every principal street, there are arches and great gates, which for each man's security are shut every night, and in most of the streets are goodly fountains whose water is excellent to drink. Besides, at every full and new moon, open fairs are kept in several places, whither merchants resort from all parts, and where there is an abundance of all kinds of foodstuffs especially meat and fruit. A great store of fish, chiefly soles and mullet, is taken in this river and is all sold alive, besides a world of sea fish, both salted, dried and fresh. We were told that there are 10,000 trades for the working of silk, which is sent all over the kingdom.

The city is surrounded with a strong wall made of fair hewed stone. There are 130 gates, at each of which there is a porter and two halberdiers, who are bound to give an account of all that passes in and out every day. There are also 12 forts or citadels with ramparts and high towers like our own, but without any cannon at all. I will not speak of the royal palace, because I only saw it from the outside.

Inland Waterways

Mendes Pinto and his companions were sent by river and canal to Peking; the journey made a great impression upon him, especially the river itself.

I will show you that one of the principal reasons why this monarchy of China, that contains 32 kingdoms, is so mighty, rich and full of trade is because it is exceedingly well supplied with rivers and a world of canals that have been anciently made by the kings, great lords and the people thereof. The narrowest of the canals has bridges over them. Moreover, all the roads from cities, towns and villages are made of fair stone, at the ends of which are costly pillars and arches with inscriptions in letters of gold, containing the praises of them that erected them.

There were floating towns on the rivers.

Now, when all these vessels come to join together during their fairs, they make a great and fair town

Thevenol. *Relation de Divers Voyages Curieux.* 1663. Bodleian Library

Chinese junks from a European travel book of 1663

sometimes a league in length and three-quarters of a league in breadth, being composed of above 20,000 vessels, besides an infinite number of small boats. There are in this moving town 2,000 streets, most of which are covered with silks and adorned with banners, flags and streamers, wherein all kinds of commodities are sold. As soon as it is night, all these streets are shut up with cords across them so that no one may pass after the curfew has sounded. In each of these streets of water there are at least a dozen lanthorns with lights burning. In every street, even the poorest, there is a chapel to pray in containing idols and priests to administer sacrifices and accept the offerings that are made to them. We beheld other ships, covered with silken hangings, where comedies and other plays were presented to entertain the people who flocked to them in great numbers. There were also vessels all laden with dead men's skulls which were bought to present as an offering at the funeral of friends, for if the dead is laid in the grave in the company of these skulls, his soul will enter heaven.

Peking

We continued our course up the river until at length on **Tuesday, the 19th of October, 1542,** we arrived at the great city of Peking. We were cast into prison where for welcome on the first day we had 30 lashes a piece given us.

Their trial dragged on for six months until they were found not guilty but were exiled to Quinsay for a year. There they were treated well and were employed as halberdiers by the Governor until there was a quarrel.

This division sprang from a vanity associated with the Portuguese nation: two of us nine fell into an

Walls of Peking about 1671 by a European artist

argument about the family trees of the Madureyras and the Fonsecas and which of these two noble houses enjoyed the most esteem at the court of the king of Portugal. The matter started with them shouting like fish-wives at each other, then one gave the other a great box on the ear, he instantly gave him a blow with a sword which cut away almost half his cheek, who feeling himself hurt caught up a halberd and therewith ran the other through the arm. In the meantime, the Cheam came running in person to this tumult and had us all arrested and gave us presently 30 lashes each.

So from a position of trust and comfort, they returned to prison once more and were set to work in the local forges. Once again, they were saved from their difficulties by an unexpected event; the Tartars (Mongols) attacked Northern China.

The next morning, a little before sunrise, the enemy appeared in most dreadful manner; they were divided up into seven great battalions, having flags quartered with green and white, which are the colours of the king of Tartary, and marched to the sound of trumpets. Having marched to within arquebus shot of the town walls, they suddenly rushed at them with hideous cries, and rearing up over 2,000 ladders, assaulted the town on all sides with invincible courage. Though the besieged made some resistance, they were unable to hinder the enemy from effecting his design: by means of certain iron rams they broke down the four main gates and rendered themselves masters of the town after slaying the Cheam together with a great number of mandarins. Thus did the barbarians possess themselves of this miserable town, all the inhabitants whereof they put to the sword without sparing any. After this bloody massacre, the town was fired, the principal houses overthrown and the most sumptuous temples levelled to the ground.

The Tartars

Shortly after this success, the Tartars (or Mongols) were defeated before the fortress of Nixianicos and Jorge Mendes, one of the Portuguese, offered his services to the Tartars in exchange for a safe conduct to the coast. The Tartar commander accepted and Mendes' plan succeeded, so that he and all the Portuguese who had taken part in the fighting were taken to the camp of the king of Tartary.

The King was sat on his throne under a rich cloth of state and had about him twelve young boys carrying silver maces like sceptres; close behind him was a young lady extremely beautiful and wonderfully attired who ever and anon fanned him. The king was about 40 years of age, of full stature, somewhat lean and of good aspect. His beard was very short, his moustaches worn in the Turkish manner (long and thin), his eyes like those of the Chinese, and his countenance severe and majestic. His clothes were violet in colour and embroidered with pearls; upon his feet he had green sandals covered with pearls; and on his head a satin cap, which was the same colour as his clothes, with a rich band of diamonds and rubies round it. After we had gone 10 or 11 steps into the room, we kissed the ground three times.

The Tartar commander described their services and they were granted a safe conduct and went with an ambassador to Cochin-China where they were offered passage to Macao, a Portuguese base in southern China, on two pirate junks. As they sailed along the Chinese coast:

It was our ill-fortune to be assailed by a pirate who with seven great junks fell to fighting with us

AMACAO.

Macao in 1598 by a European artist. What Chinese objects can you see?

from six in the morning until ten o'clock; the conflict was so fierce with shot and pots of artificial fire that three sail were burnt, two of the pirate's and one of ours, which was the junk carrying five Portugals, whom we could by no means help. But at length towards night, being helped by the afternoon's gale, it pleased our Lord that we escaped out of this pirate's hands. We continued our course for three days together, at the end of which we were encircled by so great and impetuous a storm that we lost the coast and were forced to make with full sail towards the islands of the Lequios (off Japan). We could not make land as we lacked a pilot, ours being slain in the fight, and the wind and tide were against us. We beat up and down for twenty-three days before we discovered land. We went and rode at anchor just before an island in seventy fathoms, and presently we beheld two boats coming towards us. The men in them demanded whence we came; having answered that we came from China with merchandise, intending to trade in this place if we were suffered, one replied that the Nautaquim, the lord of the island, called Tanixumaa (a small island off Kyushu) would willingly permit this upon payment of such customs as are usual in Japan, continued he.

Japan

The Nautaquim visited their ship and was struck by their looks and astonished by their history. He invited them to spend a day at his house and provided them with lodgings while the captain of their ship sold all his merchandise at a huge profit.

Having little to do, one of us, called Diogo Zeimoto, went many times a-shooting for his pleasure with an arquebus, so that going one day by chance to a certain marsh, he killed about six-and-twenty wild ducks. In the meantime these people beholding this manner of shooting, which they had never seen before, were much amazed and brought it to the notice of the Nautaquim, who not knowing what to make of this novelty sent for Zeimoto. When he saw him come with two Chinese with him carrying the fowl, he was mightily taken with the matter; for as they had never seen a gun before in that country, they all concluded that of necessity it must be some sorcery. Thereupon, Zeimoto seeing them so astonished, fired three shots for them killing a kite and two turtle-doves. The Nautaquim caused Zeimoto to get up on his horse's crupper behind him and announced: 'Know all men that the Nautaquim, prince of this island of Tanixumaa, expressly commands that all persons who inhabit the land that lies between the two seas, to honour the stranger from the furthest end of the earth for hereafter he is my kinsmen; and whosoever shall not do so, he shall be sure to lose his head.' Now Zeimoto conceived that he could not better acknowledge the honour the Nautaquim did him than by giving him the arquebus and teaching him how to make powder. Now the Nautaquim taking pleasure in nothing so much as shooting the arquebus, the Japanese drew up plans of the said arquebus to make others by it, and the effect thereof was such that before our departure (which was five and a half months later) there were six hundred of them made in the country, whereby one may perceive what the inclination of these people is, and how they are addicted to wars, wherein they take more delight than any other nation we know.

Ogilby, *Atlas Japanensis*, 1670. Bodleian Library

The arquebus, introduced by Diogo Zeimoto, was lastingly popular in Japan. This picture shows two Japanese soldiers or samurai of the 17th century each armed with an arquebus. Each soldier also has two swords.

Finally, after many more adventures, Mendes Pinto reached Malacca in 1544, only to set out on yet another voyage in a matter of weeks. This little group of Portuguese sailors was one of the earliest to penetrate Ming China and the first to reach Japan.

Adapted from *The Travels, Voyages and Adventures of Mendes Pinto* as translated by Henry Cogan in 1653.

Questions to consider

What kind of man was Mendes Pinto?

What features of Nanking impressed him most? Does his description of Nanking surprise you in any way?

What did he learn about Chinese law and punishment?

Do you think the Portuguese influence on the Japanese was good for them?

See Chapter 15 for Jenkinson's description of the Tartars (Mongols) in Russia. What differences and likenesses do you find between the Tartars in Russia and those in China?

What goods did the Chinese have that Europeans would have liked to buy?

Describe in words and pictures what life was like on the Chinese rivers.

18 The Voyages of Tasman

Throughout the Middle Ages, geographers believed that there was a great continent in the Southern hemisphere to counter-balance the land masses of the North. The Spanish and Portuguese sent out many expeditions to discover this mysterious land and much of the Pacific Ocean was explored. Towards the end of the sixteenth century, the Dutch became the strongest European power in the East and took up the search for a rich new continent. The most famous voyage was that of Abel Tasman who was the most trusted commander of Anthony van Diemen, the Governor of the Dutch Empire in the east. The idea was to sail south from Mauritius and then eastwards into the Indian Ocean. The following account is taken from Tasman's own record:

This day August 14th, 1642, we set sail from the roads of Batavia (the capital of the Dutch Empire on the island of Java) with the Yacht *Heemskerck* and the Flute* *Zeehaen*, the wind being Northeast with good weather. On the same evening the *Zeehaen* ran aground near the island of Rotterdam but got afloat again in the night without any notable damage, after which we continued our journey to the Straits of Sunda.

September 5th: In the morning we saw the island of Mauritius, steered for it and came to anchor before it at about 9 o'clock. We sent 6 sailors together with one of our second mates to the woods to assist the huntsmen there in capturing game and to bring the same to our ships. We were engaged nearly all day in repairing our ropes and tackle; as our rigging was old, weak and not to be depended upon, we added 3 more large ropes to the rigging on both sides of the main and fore masts in order to steady them.

After several weeks of repairs, the ships were ready to continue their voyage, and sailed south as planned on October 8.

Portrait of Abel Tasman

Radio Times Hulton Picture Library

* A ship specially designed as a cargo carrier.

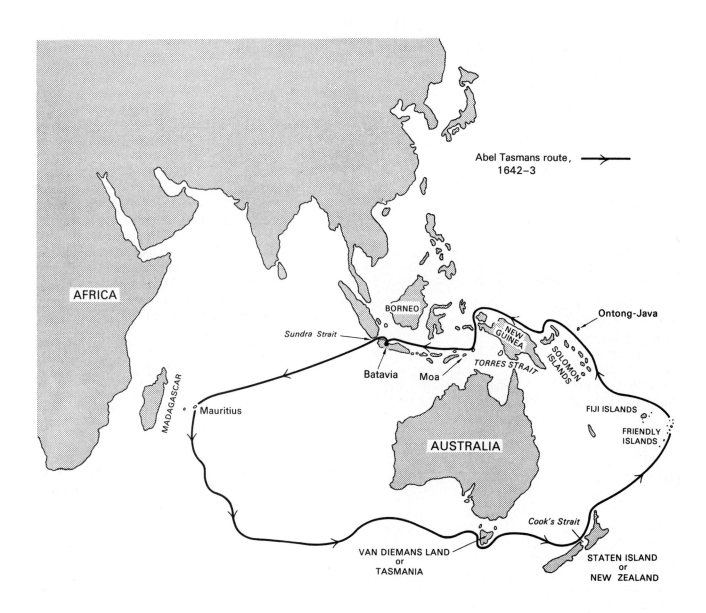

Abel Tasmans route, 1642–3 ⟶

AFRICA

BORNEO

Ontong-Java

NEW GUINEA

SOLOMON ISLANDS

Sundra Strait

Batavia

Moa

TORRES STRAIT

MADAGASCAR

Mauritius

AUSTRALIA

FIJI ISLANDS

FRIENDLY ISLANDS

Cook's Strait

VAN DIEMANS LAND
or
TASMANIA

STATEN ISLAND
or
NEW ZEALAND

October 24th: In the morning we took in our bonnets, lowered the foresail and ran on before the wind with our main sail only; we dared not try to sail to the windward (the direction from which the wind was blowing) because of the strong gale. This gale was accompanied by hail and rain to such a degree that we feared that the ship would not live through it, but at noon the storm somewhat abated so that we hauled to the wind (turned the head of the ship nearer to the point from which the wind was blowing). We could not see *Zeehaen* so we waited for her. In the morning when we sent a man to the masthead to look for her he saw her astern of which we were very glad.

They sailed south through fog and rain.

November 6th: This morning, the wind was still Westerly with hail and snow so that we had to run on with a furled foresail as before, but as we could not make any progress in this way, we deemed it best to alter course to the Northward upon which a meeting of our ship's council and our second mates decided to shape our course Northeast, running on to 45 or 44 degrees latitude. At noon our latitude was estimated at 49° 4′, and our longitude at 114° 56′.

November 24th: In the afternoon about 4 o'clock, we saw land bearing East-by-North of us at about 10 miles distance from us. At about 5 o'clock, we anchored 3 miles off shore in 60 fathoms of water with a coral bottom. This land being the first land we have met in the South Sea and not being known to any European nations, we have conferred on it the name of Anthony van Diemen's land (Tasmania) in honour of the Governor-General, our illustrious master, who sent us to make this discovery.

December 2nd: Early in the morning we sent our Pilot-major in command of our pinnace★ manned by 4 musketeers and 6 rowers, all of them armed with pikes and side-arms, together with the cockboat† of the *Zeehaen* to a bay in order to discover what facilities (fresh water, food, timber and the like) were available there. They rowed the space of upwards of a mile round the point where they found high but level ground covered with vegetation, an abundance of excellent timber and a gently sloping water-course. They heard certain human sounds resembling the music of a trumpet or gong not far from them, though they had seen no one. They saw two trees about 12 to 15 feet in thickness whose lowest branches were 60 to 65 feet from the ground. The trees bore notches made by flint tools, forming steps to enable persons to get up the trees and rob the birds' nests in their tops; as the steps were fully 5 feet apart our men concluded that the natives here must be very tall. A short time before we sighted our boats returning to the ships, we saw dense smoke arising from the land; when our men came on board again, we enquired whether they had made a fire but they said no, so there can be no doubt that there are men of extraordinary stature here.

After cruising along the east coast of Tasmania, it was decided to sail due east to make further discoveries (December 5) so that Tasman did not reach Southern Australia.

December 13th: Towards noon, we saw a large, high lying land (New Zealand) bearing Southeast of us at about 15 miles distance. We made straight for this land.

★ Usually a small two masted sailing vessel.
† A cockboat was a small oared ship's boat.

They did not anchor and sailed cautiously along the coast.

December 18th: Two boats put out to us from the shore and the men in the prows called to us in rough hollow voices, but we could not understand a word they said. They also blew several times on an instrument like a Moorish trumpet so we ordered one of our sailors who had some knowledge of trumpet blowing to play them some tunes in answer. After this had been repeated several times on both sides and it was getting dark, the natives ceased and paddled off.

December 19th: Early in the morning a boat manned by 13 natives approached; these people were of ordinary height, they had rough voices and strong bones, the colour of their skin was between brown and yellow, they wore tufts of black hair upon the tops of their heads which were tied at the back in the manner of the Japanese, surmounted by a large, white feather. Their boats consisted of two long, narrow hulls set side by side, over which a number of planks and seats were placed in such a way that those above can see through them to the water beneath; their paddles were upwards of six feet in length, narrow and pointed at one end—they could travel at considerable speeds in these vessels. For clothing, some of them wore mats, others cotton stuffs; almost all of them were naked from the shoulders to the waist. We repeatedly made signs for them to come on board but they paddled back to the shore. We saw 7 more boats put off from the shore. The skipper of the *Zeehaen* (who was with us on board the *Heemskerck*) sent off his quartermaster in the cockboat with orders to his second mate not to allow too many natives aboard. While the cockboat was paddling to the *Zeehaen*, one canoe paddled furiously towards it and struck it so

A drawing from Tasman's log. There is a canoe of the Nev[…] of December 19th is shown in the background.

violently that it gave a great lurch; upon which the foremost villain in this canoe thrust the quartermaster in the neck several times with so much force that the poor man fell overboard. The other

A. Zijn onze Schepen
B. Zijn de prauwen die om ns boort quamen
C. n des Zeehaens prauwen dat na ons boort quam Schepen in Vijn Jisuon dies des landes vermeestert in dat nat doort Schieten Woldorm Platcis heeft doen wij Zagen dat Zy de Prauwen Velacht hadden in onze Schepen met onze Shalous Woboom gehaelt
D. n' de Wothoningh Van hose prauwen in het Zatzen Vant
E. Zijn onze Schepen die onder Zeijle gaen
F. is onze Shaloup die de Prauwen Wobom haelt

aland Maoris in the foreground. The battle

Tasman, Journal, 1898. British Museum. photo P. Davey

natives fell upon the men in the cockboat with short thick clubs and overcame them—3 of our men were killed and a fourth was mortally wounded. The quartermaster and two sailors swam to our ship. We and those on board the *Zeehaen* fired our muskets and guns but did not hit any of them. We weighed anchor and set sail, since we could not hope to enter into friendly relations with these people. This is the second land which we have sailed along and discovered. In honour of the States-General (the Dutch Parliament), we gave this discovery the name of Staten Land.

December 20th: At first we had thought that this land was an island and had expected to find a passage through to the South Sea, but to our grievous disappointment it proved otherwise. The wind being Westerly, we did our best to get out of the bay by the same passage we had entered, but the sea ran very strongly into this bay and we could make no headway.

1643 January 4th: Towards noon we were drifting in a calm when we found ourselves in the midst of a very strong current, which drove us to westward. There was besides a heavy sea running from the Northeast which gave us great hopes of finding a passage there.

If they had sailed further to the east, they would have discovered a passage, which is now known as Cook's Strait, but instead they sailed northeast until they sighted Tonga-tabu, the principal island of the group called the Friendly Islands.

January 21st: In the morning we sailed to the Northwest of the island (Tonga-Tabu) where we dropped anchor in 25 fathoms with a coral bottom. About noon a small canoe with 3 men in it put off and came near our ship. We showed them some white linen and made them presents of a small Chinese looking-glass and a string of beads before they paddled ashore again. Shortly afterwards a

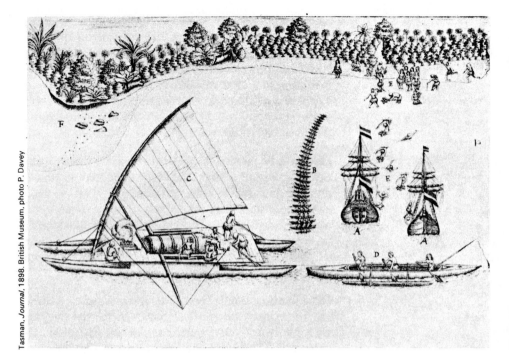

Tasman, *Journal*, 1898. British Museum, photo P. Davey

left: Tasman's drawing of a bay in the Friendly Islands—he shows two different kinds of boats belonging to the islanders, and two Dutch ships. Why do you think there is a fire and a shelter in the boat on the left?

Right: Tasman's drawing of islanders in Moa in the East Indies

great number of canoes came alongside containing cocoa-nuts for which we exchanged old nails. After some time an aged man came on board to whom the others paid homage so we concluded he was their chief. We conducted him to the main cabin and presented him with a knife, a small looking glass and some cloth. As we were leaving the cabin one of the natives was caught in the act of stealing the skipper's pistol and a pair of slippers. We took these from him without showing the least sign of dissatisfaction. Many of these people have the lower part of the body down to the knees painted black, some have a mother-of-pearl shell hanging on the breast. Towards evening 20 canoes came alongside bringing a present from the king, consisting of a fine large hog, a number of cocoa-nuts and some jams.

From the Friendly Islands, they made their way to the Fijis which they reached on February 6. Here, they held a ship's council which decided that they should sail Northwestwards for New Guinea. On this leg of their journey, they visited some islands off the Solomons which they named Ontong-Java. Not all their visits were fruitful; this is what happened at the Groene Islands.

March 29th: Half-way through the afternoon, two small canoes came alongside; they had two wings or outriggers, their paddles were small and

thick in the blade and poorly made it seemed to us. When they were about 2 ships' lengths from us, one made signs of peace. These men were stark naked, their bodies black with curly hair, their noses were flat. Some wore white bracelets of what seemed to be bone, others had their faces daubed with lime. They carried nothing but bows and arrows and short spears. We presented them with 2 strings of beads and 2 large nails, and in return they gave us one old cocoa-nut which was all we had from them!

On April 1, New Guinea was sighted and a few days later Tasman wrote:

We felt so violent an earthquake shock that none of our men, however sound asleep, remained in his hammock, but all came running on deck thinking the ship had struck a rock.

After this excitement, they continued along the coast of New Guinea, and passed through the Straits of Gilolo and visited the island of Moa:

May 3rd: This morning several canoes came alongside while our men were engaged in washing the deck. One of the sailors, who was standing on the whales (the great timbers running the whole length of the ship) to hand up a bucket of water, was shot at and hit in the thick part of the leg above the thigh by an arrow, we immediately replied with our muskets so that one of the natives was hit in the arm. They sent on board the man who had shot the arrow to make his peace which he did.

They completed their voyage by sailing through the seas of Banda, Flores and Java to Batavia. Tasman concluded his account with this entry:

June 15th: In the morning at daybreak I went to Batavia in the pinnace. God be praised and thanked for this happy voyage. Amen.

It has been said that Tasman's expedition provided the greatest advance in geographical knowledge since Magellan's voyage.

The Governor-General and the Councillors at Batavia agreed that it was 'a remarkable voyage' but complained that Tasman:

had been to some extent remiss in investigating the situation, the conformation and the nature of the lands and peoples discovered, and had left the main part of this task to be executed by some inquisitive successor.

As a result of this voyage, it was thought for some time that New Guinea, Australia (parts of which had been visited by earlier Dutch explorers) and Tasmania all formed part of a great continental island which was believed to be separated by sea from the Southern Continent. Tasman tried to clear up some of the remaining questions by another voyage in 1644 when he visited Northern Australia, but once again he failed to make one of the crucial discoveries, that of the strait between Australia and New Guinea. His pioneering work was followed up by William Dampier and Captain Cook.

Adapted from *The Journal of his Discovery of Van Dieman's Land by Abel Tasman* translated (1898 edition).

Suggestions for practical work

1. Make a series of models or drawings of the canoes used by the islanders of the Pacific. How did those of the Maoris and the Friendly Islanders differ?
2. Write an illustrated account of the Maoris.

Questions to consider

How well were Tasman's ships prepared for a long and dangerous voyage?

What evidence did the Dutchmen find that Tasmania was inhabited?

What can you find out about the Maoris and the Moan islanders from Tasman's drawings?

Why was Tasman so successful in avoiding trouble with the various islanders?

Do you think that Abel Tasman was as great a seaman as the other captains you have studied? Give your reasons.

Imagine that you sailed with Tasman. Write a diary of the voyage.

Index

Cover painting: 'Dutch ships returning down to a rocky shore' by Ertvelt reproduced by courtesy of the National Maritime Museum, London.